BANGLADESH 2016 HUMAN RIGHTS REPORT

EXECUTIVE SUMMARY

Bangladesh is a secular, pluralistic, parliamentary democracy. Prime Minister Sheikh Hasina and the Awami League (AL) have retained power since the January 2014 parliamentary elections, which most international observers characterized as controversial and falling short of international standards.

Civilian authorities maintained effective control over the security forces.

Extremist organizations claiming affiliation with Da'esh and al-Qaida in the Indian Subcontinent (AQIS) increased their activities in the country, executing high-profile attacks on religious minorities; academics; foreigners; human rights activists; lesbian, gay, bisexual, transgender, and intersex (LGBTI) community members; and other groups. The government responded with a strong anti-militancy drive, which human rights groups claim has resulted in increased extrajudicial killings, arbitrary detentions for the purpose of extortion, enforced disappearances, torture, and other abuses of human rights. The government further used counterterrorism efforts to justify restrictions of civil and political rights.

The most significant human rights problems were extrajudicial killings, arbitrary or unlawful detentions, and forced disappearances by government security forces; the killing of members of marginalized groups and others by groups espousing extremist views; early and forced marriage; gender-based violence, especially against women and children; and poor working conditions and labor rights abuses.

Other human rights problems included torture and abuse by security forces; arbitrary arrests; weak judicial capacity and independence; lengthy pretrial detentions; politically motivated violence; official corruption; and restrictions on online speech and the press. Authorities infringed on citizens' privacy rights. Some nongovernmental organizations (NGOs) faced continued legal and informal restrictions on their activities. Discrimination against persons with disabilities was a problem, especially for children seeking admission to public school. Instances of societal violence against religious and ethnic minorities persisted. Discrimination against persons based on their sexual orientation increased.

There were reports of widespread impunity for security force abuses. The government took limited measures to investigate and prosecute cases of abuse and killing by security forces, including through the Internal Enquiry Cell of the Rapid

Action Battalion (RAB). Public distrust of police and security services deterred many from approaching government forces for assistance or to report criminal incidents. In several instances, the government blamed victims of extremist attacks, increasing the impunity of attackers.

Section 1. Respect for the Integrity of the Person, Including Freedom from:

a. Arbitrary Deprivation of Life and other Unlawful or Politically Motivated Killings

The constitution provides for the rights to life and personal liberty. Media and local and international human rights organizations reported the government or its agents committed numerous arbitrary or unlawful killings.

Suspicious deaths occurred during raids, arrests, and other law enforcement operations. Often security forces claimed they took a suspect in custody to a crime scene or hideout late at night to recover weapons or identify conspirators and that the suspect was killed when his conspirators shot at police. The government usually described these deaths as "crossfire killings," "gunfights," or "encounter killings," terms used to characterize exchanges of gunfire between RAB or police units and criminal gangs, although the media sometimes also used these terms to describe legitimate uses of police force. Human rights organizations and media outlets claimed many of these "crossfire" incidents actually constituted extrajudicial killings (EJKs), In some cases, human rights organizations claimed that law enforcement units would detain, interrogate, and torture suspects, bring them back to the scene of the original arrest, execute them, and ascribe the death to lawful self-defense in response to violent attacks. One human rights organization reported that 150 individuals were killed in "crossfire" incidents in the first nine months of the year, including 34 by RAB, 11 by the Detective Branch of police, one by the Bangladesh Border Guard (BGB), three in a joint SWAT operation, and 61 by other police forces. Another human rights organization reported that security forces killed 118 individuals in the first nine months of the year.

Authorities claim that on August 5 a suspected Islamic extremist named Shafiul Islam Don was killed in a gunfight that occurred when attackers fired on a RAB vehicle transporting the suspect. RAB officials claim that Don confessed in custody to participating in a July 7 attack on an Eid ceremony in Sholakia. Similarly, Ghulam Faijullaha Fahim died in police custody on June 18 when officers allegedly took him to capture his associates, who then attacked police. Local persons had apprehended Fahim when he attempted to attack a mathematics teacher on June 15, and they turned him over to police. Other suspects were killed when police tried to apprehend them. For example, on June 19 police killed Shariful Islam Shihab, a suspect in the murder of the blogger Avijit Roy. Authorities stated that Shariful and two accomplices opened fire on the police as they tried to flee on a motorbike; the two accomplices reportedly escaped.

Although not as numerous or widespread as 2015, politically motivated killings continued by both members of the ruling and opposition parties. A human rights organization reported that political violence resulted in 209 deaths. Violence committed by student and youth wings of political parties was a problem. Violence also occurred between supporters of the ruling party. In July, one person died when two factions of the Bangladesh Chhatra League clashed at Comilla University over placing wreaths at the portrait of founding leader Sheikh Mujibur Rahman.

As of October, groups claiming affiliation with transnational terrorist organizations, including Da'esh and AQIS, claimed to have killed 39 individuals, including members of religious minorities, academics, foreigners, LGBTI activists, and members of security forces. Another 31 attacks were unclaimed. Members of the Hindu minority population constituted a significant portion of the victims.

b. Disappearance

Human rights groups and media reported that multiple disappearances and kidnappings continued, some committed by security services. The government made limited efforts to prevent or investigate such acts. The United Nations Working Group on Enforced or Involuntary Disappearances contacted the government on March 9 concerning the "reportedly alarming rise of the number of cases of enforced disappearances in the country" and had 34 outstanding cases under review as of May 18, but the working group did not receive a response. Following alleged disappearances, security forces released some individuals without charge, arrested some, some were found dead, and others were never found. A human rights organization claimed that individuals in law enforcement uniforms or claiming to be law enforcement "kidnapped" 84 individuals in the first 11 months of the year. Targets of disappearances included individuals affiliated with opposition political parties.

On the night of August 22, Abdullahil Amaan Azmi, son of convicted war criminal and former Jamaat leader Ghulam Azam, was allegedly abducted from his Dhaka apartment by men in plain clothes who reportedly identified themselves as members of the Detective Branch. Unlike his father, Azmi was never an official member of Jamaat. He is a known figure in Bangladesh politics and active on social media, however, and his Facebook posts were often critical of the government. Similarly, on August 9, Mir Ahmed Bin Quasem, son of top Jamaat leader and convicted war criminal Mir Quasem Ali, was allegedly abducted. Mir Ahmed had been serving as the legal representative for Jamaat until his abduction. On August 4, Hummam Quader Chowdhury, son of senior Bangladesh Nationalist Party (BNP) leader and executed war criminal Salauddin Quader Chowdhury, was also reportedly picked up by unidentified men. They are widely reported to remain in government detention.

c. Torture and Other Cruel, Inhuman, or Degrading Treatment or Punishment

Although the constitution and law prohibit torture and other cruel, inhuman, or degrading treatment or punishment, local and international human rights organizations and the media reported security forces, including RAB, intelligence services, and police, employed torture and physical and psychological abuse during arrests and interrogations. Security forces reportedly used torture to gather information from alleged militants although members of political opposition parties claimed that security forces also targeted activists within their parties. Security forces reportedly used threats, beatings, kneecappings, and electric shock, and law enforcement officers sometimes committed rapes and other sexual abuses. Two prominent human rights organizations stated that security forces tortured eight persons to death in the first nine months of the year.

The law contains provisions allowing a magistrate to place a suspect in interrogative custody, known as remand, during which questioning of the suspect can take place without a lawyer present. Human rights organizations alleged that many instances of torture occur during this remand period as a means of obtaining information from the suspect. On November 10, the Supreme Court issued guidelines for arrest without warrant and interrogation of suspects on remand, aimed at preventing legal detention of citizens not charged with a crime. In its bid to reduce custodial torture, the court issued guidelines for law enforcement personnel as well as the courts regarding medical checks for detainees on remand and probes into allegations of torture. The court also asked the government to amend certain sections of the Criminal Procedure Code (CrPC) to reduce police abuse of citizens (see section 1.d).

A human rights organization claimed that law enforcement personnel shot 16 detainees in the legs during the first 11 months of the year. A Human Rights Watch report released in September detailed the cases of 25 individuals shot in the legs by security forces since 2013, including one case in 2016 when a news reporter and human rights organization volunteer Mohammad Afzal Hossain was shot in the leg by security forces while reporting on voting irregularities in an election between two Awami league candidates in Rajapur. On January 15, Anwar Hossain Mahbub, Joint Secretary of a ward-level BNP unit, was arrested and allegedly tortured in prison, leading to his death on February 16. Idris Ali, a madrassa teacher and two-time local council chairman candidate for Jamaat, was reportedly kidnapped by plain-clothes security officials on August 4 and found dead on August 12 with alleged signs of torture, including broken hands and legs and cut tendons. On June 8, police in Jessore reportedly tortured a 16-year-old boy named Ainul Haque Rohit for allegedly stealing a motorbike. A human rights organization stated that police detained Rohit for 30 hours during which they blindfolded him; beat his joints, fingers, toes, and soles of his feet with a wooden rod; stuffed his vest in his mouth; and poured water in his nose for 10 minutes. The police reportedly released Rohit after receiving a bribe from his family. There was no accountability for these specific actions, and the government rarely charged, convicted, or punished those responsible for similar abuses.

Security forces at times committed rape and other sexual abuse of detainees and others. On May 22, assistant sub-inspector Delwar Hossain of Dagonbhuiyan Police Station, with assistance from officer Abdul Mannan, raped a woman who went to the station to file a complaint over a family dispute. The woman later filed a case under the Women and Children Repression Prevention Act and the authorities brought the two men to court, where they were found guilty and sent to prison.

Starting in January, the government investigated allegations that two Bangladeshi peacekeepers sexually abused a minor in the Central African Republic in 2015. One was dismissed from service and sentenced to one year in prison, and the allegations against the second peacekeeper were found to be unsubstantiated. The government continues to investigate an allegation, which came to light in February 2016, that a Bangladeshi peacekeeper sexually exploited an adult in the Democratic Republic of the Congo in late 2015/early 2016. The government made the example of the peacekeeper sentenced for sexual abuse in the Central African Republic available as part of an awareness-raising campaign and incorporated it into the pretraining peacekeeping deployment curriculum.

Prison and Detention Center Conditions

Prison conditions remained harsh and at times life threatening due to overcrowding, inadequate facilities, and lack of proper sanitation. Odhikar stated these conditions contributed to custodial deaths, with 54 prisoners dying in prison in the first 11 months of the year.

<u>Physical Conditions</u>: According to the Department of Prisons, in October there were 78,578 prisoners in a system designed to hold 36,614 inmates. Authorities often incarcerated pretrial detainees with convicted prisoners.

Due to overcrowding, prisoners slept in shifts and did not have adequate toilet facilities. According to GIZ, the prisons do not meet minimum standards for adequate light, air, decency, and privacy. Human rights organizations and the media stated some prisoners did not receive medical care or water although prison authorities stated that each prison has access to water. Water available in prisons was comparable with water available in the rest of the country, which was frequently not potable. Human Rights Commission Chairman Kazi Reazul Hoque told the media on August 23 after visiting the newly built Dhaka Central Jail in Keraniganj that human rights are being violated in the prison. He further said, "We will visit the prison every three months to improve the situation." Despite the new facility, there were still problems there. Prisoners at the new Dhaka Central Jail told the media in May that they must pay approximately 30,000 taka ($381) per month for food, bathing and toilet use, places to sleep, and other services. Authorities reportedly charged additional fees for visits with family members.

Conditions in prisons, and often within the same prison complex, varied widely, because authorities lodged some prisoners in areas subject to high temperatures, poor ventilation, and overcrowding. The law allows individuals designated as VIPs to access "division A" prison facilities with improved living conditions and food, more frequent family visitation rights, and provision of a poorer prisoner to serve as an aide in their cell.

While the law requires holding juveniles separately from adults, many juveniles were incarcerated with adults. Children were sometimes imprisoned (occasionally with their mothers) despite laws and court decisions prohibiting the imprisonment of minors.

Authorities routinely held female prisoners separately from men. Although the law prohibits women in "safe custody" (usually victims of rape, trafficking, and domestic violence) from being housed with criminals, officials did not always provide separate facilities. Women were not permitted to leave this custody without permission from the authorities.

Although Dhaka's new central jail has facilities for people with mental disabilities, specific provisions generally do not exist for people with disabilities. Judges may, however, reduce punishments for persons with more significant disabilities on humanitarian grounds and jailors may make special arrangements, for example, transferring inmates with more significant disabilities to the prison hospital. The prison hospital accommodates people with physical disabilities, the elderly, and those with broken limbs and cardiac problems, among other issues.

Administration: There were no prison ombudsmen for prisoners to submit complaints. Prison authorities indicated that they are constrained by significant staff shortages. The scope for retraining and rehabilitation programs was extremely limited.

Independent Monitoring: The government permitted visits from the International Committee of the Red Cross and assistance from some international donors. The government allowed the Bangladesh Red Crescent Society to visit foreign detainees. Government-appointed committees composed of prominent private citizens in each prison locality monitored prisons monthly but did not publicly release their findings. District judges occasionally visited prisons.

Improvements: On July 29, prison authorities transferred 6,511 inmates from the 200-year old Dhaka Central Jail to a new location in Keraniganj on the outskirts of Dhaka. The new facility was built to accommodate 4,590 inmates, meaning the new facility was immediately overcrowded, but less so than the old jail. Those on trial are housed in six buildings while convicts are in two similar structures. Four buildings house more dangerous criminals, such as those convicted of violent crime, militants, and terrorists. There are 16 special cells for VIP prisoners, which include current and former ministers, members of parliament, senior civil servants, and individuals of similar status.

The new jail has facilities for 200 female inmates, 100 male adolescents, 40 female adolescents, 30 male prisoners with mental disabilities, and 20 female prisoners with mental disabilities. The jail has 60 classified wards and 400 cells for dangerous prisoners. The new jail also has a 200-bed hospital and a daycare center.

Other facilities, such as the Old Dhaka Central Jail, have poorer light, sanitation, ventilation, and other conditions and do not meet UN/Mandela standards.

d. Arbitrary Arrest or Detention

The constitution prohibits arbitrary arrest and detention. The law permits authorities to arrest and detain persons suspected of criminal activity without an order from a magistrate or a warrant. Authorities sometimes held detainees without a charge sheet, without divulging their whereabouts or circumstances to family or legal counsel, or without acknowledging having arrested them in the first place.

Role of the Police and Security Apparatus

Police, who fall under the jurisdiction of the Ministry of Home Affairs (MOHA), have a mandate to maintain internal security and law and order. The Police Special Branch enforces immigration law while the BGB and the Bangladesh Coast Guard (BCG)--also under MOHA--enforce the country's borders. Both Dhaka Metropolitan Police's Detective Branch and the Criminal Investigation Department conduct investigations. The Counter Terrorism and Transnational Crime Unit, which began operating during the year under the Dhaka Metropolitan Police but has now nationwide jurisdiction, has taken a leading role in counterterrorism efforts. RAB, composed of forces drawn from the police and military, also has a counterterrorism role in addition to other duties. The military, organized under the Prime Minister's Office, is responsible for external security, but it can be called to help as a back-up force with a variety of domestic security responsibilities when required in aid to civil authority. This includes responding to instances of terrorism. For example, elite military units based in Chittagong and Sylhet traveled to Dhaka to support local police to end an 11-hour terrorism hostage incident on July 1. The Directorate General of Forces Intelligence and National Security Intelligence are the primary means by which the government gathers information on topics of interest, including national security matters.

Civilian authorities maintained effective control over the military and other security forces, and the government has mechanisms to investigate and punish abuse and corruption within the security forces. These mechanisms were not regularly employed, however. The government took steps to improve police professionalism, discipline, training, and responsiveness and to reduce corruption. Police basic training continued to incorporate instruction on the appropriate use of force as part of efforts to implement community-based policing.

According to police policy, all significant uses of force by police, including actions that resulted in serious physical injury or death, trigger an automatic internal investigation, usually by a professional standards unit that reports directly to the Inspector General of Police (IGP). The government, however, neither released statistics on total killings by security personnel nor took comprehensive measures to investigate cases despite previous statements by high-ranking officials that the government would show "zero tolerance" and fully investigate all extrajudicial killings by security forces that occurred in 2016. Some human rights groups expressed skepticism over the independence of the professional standards units conducting these assessments. In the few known instances in which the government brought charges, those found guilty generally received only administrative punishment. Some members of the security forces acted with impunity. For example, authorities did not make progress in a case regarding the alleged rape and murder of Sohagi Jahan Tonu, a second-year student of Comilla Victoria College, whose body was discovered March 20 in the Comilla military cantonment, a military base where she lived with her family. Tonu's parents alleged that an army sergeant and a soldier committed the act. Despite two autopsies including DNA samples, authorities have not arrested the perpetrators, which sparked widespread condemnation and student protests. In another case, on November 13 a court in Kushtia issued arrest warrants for three policemen, including an officer in charge, for allegedly killing a farmer in a "crossfire" in 2007 after they tried unsuccessfully to extort money from his family.

Despite such efforts, security forces, including RAB, continued to commit abuses with impunity. Plaintiffs were reluctant to accuse police in criminal cases due to lengthy trial procedures and fear of retribution. Reluctance to bring charges against police also perpetuated a climate of impunity. Officers loyal to the ruling party occupied many of the key positions in the law enforcement agencies.

The government continued support of an Internal Enquiry Cell (IEC) within the paramilitary unit RAB that investigates cases of human rights abuses. The IEC investigated 12 cases during the year compared to 16 the previous year. The most common complaints in the 63 cases investigated since 2012 were "abuse of authority," physical harassment, and bribery. Of the 63 cases since 2012, the IEC confirmed the truth of allegations of abuse in 20 cases. As of December 2016, RAB has two cases under active review, including one investigation the IEC self-initiated following media reporting.

Security forces failed to prevent societal violence (see section 6).

Arrest Procedures and Treatment of Detainees

Police may arrest individuals on a court-issued warrant, on observation of a crime in progress, or in an attempt to preserve security and public order under the Special Powers Act. The government or a district magistrate may order a person detained for 30 days to prevent the commission of an act that could threaten national security; however, authorities sometimes held detainees for longer periods. A magistrate must inform a detainee of the grounds for detention within 15 days, and regulations require an advisory board to examine a detainee's case after four months. Detainees have the right to appeal.

On May 24, the Appellate Panel of the Supreme Court upheld an April 7, 2003, High Court decision ordering the government to amend sections 54 and 167 of the CrPC, which permit arrests without warrant and interrogation in custody known as "remand." The Appellate Panel in its full verdict released on November 10 issued guidelines for application of these sections, which will be binding on all courts and authorities (see Section 1.d and 1.c). Pending issuance of the guidelines, government security forces continued to detain citizens without a warrant and subordinate courts granted "remand" for interrogation without following safeguards established by the High Court in its 2003 verdict.

The highest court's guidelines issued on November 10 for the law enforcement agencies include preparation of a memorandum of arrest with signature of the arrested person with date and time. Police must inform a relative or a friend of the arrest within 12 hours, and enter in a diary the ground of the arrest, the name of the relative or friend who has been informed, and the name of the officer who has custody of the arrested person. The officer must show his/her identity card to the person arrested and others present during the arrest. The guidelines made official registration of a criminal case with the court essential for holding a detainee in law enforcement or judicial custody and specifically ordered a halt to arrest under Section 54 for the purpose of detention under the Special Powers Act. Under the guidelines, the officer who makes the arrest must record any visible injury on the person arrested and reasons for such injury, take the person to the nearest hospital for treatment, and obtain a certificate from the attending doctor. The guidelines stipulate a written report be given to an arrestee's relative or friend within 12 hours of arrest. If an investigation cannot be completed within 24 hours, the officer must explain why not if they want to continue to hold a suspect without a court order, and why the accusation or information against the person is considered well founded. The officer must also transmit a copy of the relevant case diary to the court.

The guidelines for judicial magistrates require them to release an arrested person if he/she is produced before the court with a petition for detention without producing a copy of the entries in the diary made during the arrest. Magistrates are required to reject the petitions of police officers if the arrested person is not produced before the court or if the allegations were not "well founded." The magistrates cannot allow remand of any arrested person for more than 15 days and could prosecute law enforcement officers under the Torture and Custodial Death (Prohibition) Act 2009 if a medical board finds evidence of custodial torture or death (see section 1.c)

There is a functioning bail system in the regular courts. Authorities granted criminal detainees charged with crimes access to attorneys. The government sometimes provided detainees with state-funded defense attorneys. The few legal aid programs for detainees that existed were underfunded. Authorities generally permitted defense lawyers to meet with their clients only after formal charges were filed in the courts, which in some cases occurred weeks or months after the initial arrest.

Despite a May 9 explicit directive from the Supreme Court's Appellate Division prohibiting rearrest of accused persons when they are released on bail and arresting them in new cases without producing them in court, police routinely used these mechanisms to detain suspects indefinitely. Media report that Jamaat's assistant secretary for Dhaka city Shafiqul Islam Masud was originally arrested in August 2014, and rearrested at the gate of Dhaka Central Jail twice, on December 25, 2015 and April 24, 2016, immediately after having received bail in more than 50 cases relating to violence during general strikes.

Arbitrary Arrest: Arbitrary arrests occurred, often in conjunction with political demonstrations, or as part of security force responses to terrorist activity, and the government held persons in detention without specific charges, sometimes in an attempt to collect information about other suspects. Police engaged in a mass arrest campaign from June 10 to 16 before the Eid holidays during which security forces reportedly arrested 14,000 individuals, including a purported 2,000 opposition-party activists. Although some government spokespersons justified the effort as an anti-militancy drive following killings of secular bloggers and religious minority leaders, security forces reportedly detained approximately 150 confirmed militants. Human rights organizations and other observers asserted that the arrest campaign largely served as a means for police to raise money through bribes and bail from arrested individuals, and to intimidate members of political opposition groups. Following the July 1 terrorist attack on Holey Bakery, security forces detained two of the released hostages, Hasnat Karim and Tahmid Khan, for their alleged role in the attack. Human rights organizations assert that unknown security forces secretly detained the two individuals for interrogation for 34 days before police officially arrested them although the government denied this allegation.

Pretrial Detention: Arbitrary and lengthy pretrial detention continued to be a problem due to bureaucratic inefficiencies, limited resources, lax enforcement of pretrial rules, and corruption. According to court sources, approximately three million civil and criminal cases were pending in 2016. In some cases, the length of pretrial detention equaled or exceeded the sentence for the alleged crime. Seventy-four percent of detainees were in pretrial detention or undergoing trial. A media report in October stated that more than 500 prisoners have spent more than five years in prison without trial. For example, authorities detained a prisoner named Shipon for more than 17 years without trial in a murder case until he was finally released on November 15 due to media attention to his case.

Observers further stated that a high-level government official pressured lawyers to decline to represent the individuals due to government interest in the case. Tahmid was granted bail on October 2, but Hasnat remained in prison at the end of the year. Authorities denied Hasnat temporary bail to attend the funeral of his father in November.

e. Denial of Fair Public Trial

The law provides for an independent judiciary, but corruption, political interference, and a substantial backlog of cases hindered the court system. A provision of the constitution that accords the executive branch authority over judicial appointments to lower courts and over compensation and assignments for judicial officials undermines full judicial independence. The 16th constitutional amendment giving parliament impeachment power over high court judges was passed in 2014, but in August the High Court found it to be unconstitutional.

Corruption and a substantial backlog of cases hindered the court system, and the granting of extended continuances effectively prevented many defendants from obtaining fair trials due to witness tampering, victim intimidation, and missing evidence. Human rights observers stated that magistrates, attorneys, and court officials demanded bribes from defendants in many cases, or ruled based on influence by or loyalty to political patronage networks. Observers noted that judges who made decisions unfavorable to the government risked being transferred to other jurisdictions. There were allegations of political influence over court decisions.

The Bangladeshi International Crimes Tribunal (ICT) continued to prosecute individuals indicted for committing war crimes during the 1971 independence war. On May 11, authorities executed Matiur Rahman Nizami, Amir (president) of Jamaat, the country's largest Islamist party, at Dhaka central jail. On September 3, authorities executed another Jamaat leader, Mir Quasem Ali, at Kashimpur prison in Gazipur. The defendants claimed that the court process was tainted by irregularities, and that the judges ignored exculpatory evidence. In total, five individuals were executed by the ICT since it was established in 2010--four from Jamaat and one from BNP.

Trial Procedures

The law provides for the right to a fair public trial, but the judiciary did not always protect this right due to corruption, partisanship, and weak personnel and institutional capacities. Lower court judges received base pay from 30,935 taka ($386) to 78,000 taka ($975) per month, depending on seniority. A High Court division judge of the Supreme Court receives a monthly base pay of 95,000 taka ($1,213) and an appellate division judge is paid 100,000 taka ($1,277). Lower court prosecutors' low monthly retainer of 3,000 taka ($37.50) plus 200 taka ($2.50) per day spent in court led some to accept bribes to influence the outcome of a case.

Defendants are presumed innocent and have the right to appeal and to see the government's evidence. Defendants also have the right to be informed promptly and in detail of the charges against them. The Speedy Trial Act was intended to prevent undue delay of proceedings for certain offenses, such as murder, sexual assault, and robbery, but frequent adjournments contributed to the backlog of cases. The accused are entitled to be present at their public trial where judges decide cases. Indigent defendants have the right to a public defender. Trials are conducted in the Bengali language and free interpretation is not provided by the government. Defendants also have the right to adequate time to prepare a defense. Accused persons have the right to representation by counsel, review accusatory material, call and question witnesses, and appeal verdicts. The government frequently did not respect these rights, and some government officials reportedly discouraged lawyers from representing defendants in controversial cases important to the state.

Mobile courts headed by executive branch magistrates rendered immediate verdicts that often included prison terms to defendants who were not afforded the opportunity for legal representation. In a July 26-28 conference in Dhaka, Deputy Commissioners from all 64 districts requested that the government expedite the passage of an amendment to the Mobile Court Act of 2009 giving the executive magistrates increased judicial powers. The act had not moved forward by the end of the year.

On September 20, the High Court summoned an executive magistrate and the officer in charge of a police station in Tangail district to investigate their use of a mobile court to jail a boy using the Information and Communication Technology (ICT) Act, which is not within the jurisdiction of the mobile courts. Media had reported that the boy was sentenced to prison for two years for a Facebook posting criticizing a local AL Member of Parliament (MP). Appearing before the High Court on September 27, the boy said the MP hit him, the officer in charge beat him, and the executive magistrate kicked him. Under the threat of being killed in "crossfire," the boy admitted to threatening the MP in the Facebook post. On October 18, the High Court declared the mobile court's decision illegal, acquitting the boy of charges and directing the secretaries of Public Administration and Home Affairs and the police to withdraw the officer in charge and the executive magistrate so they could be investigated. On October 26, the Supreme Court stayed the order to withdraw the individuals after they petitioned the court.

Political Prisoners and Detainees

There were reports of political prisoners or detainees. Political affiliation at times appeared to be a factor in the arrest and prosecution of members of the opposition parties, including through spurious charges under the pretext of responding to national security threats. Former prime minister Khaleda Zia, chairperson of the largest opposition political party, was charged with sedition for her public comment on the number of individuals people killed during the 1971 War of Independence. The government has not detained her pending trial. Opposition party members claimed that security forces arrested approximately 2,000 of their members during mass arrests in early June, although in general they were not charged or imprisoned; some were reportedly released after paying bribes.

Civil Judicial Procedures and Remedies

Individuals and organizations may seek administrative and judicial remedies for human rights violations; however, the civil court system was slow, cumbersome, and marked by public distrust, deterring many from filing complaints. The government did not interfere with civil judicial procedures. Corruption and outside influence were problems in the civil judicial system. Alternative dispute resolution for civil cases allowed citizens to present their cases for mediation. According to government sources, the wider use of mediation in civil cases accelerated the administration of justice, but there was no assessment of its fairness or impartiality.

Property Restitution

The government did not amend the 2001 Vested Property (Return) Act to accelerate the process of return of land to primarily Hindu individuals (see section 2.d.). The Vested Property Act allows the government to confiscate property of anyone that the government declares to be an enemy of the state. It was often used to seize property abandoned by minority religious groups when they fled the country, particularly after the 1971 independence war.

Minority communities reported many land ownership disputes that disproportionately displaced minorities, especially in areas near new roads or industrial development zones where land prices had recently increased. They also claimed that local police, civil authorities, and political leaders were sometimes involved or shielded politically influential land grabbers from prosecution (see section 6.). In August, the government amended the Chittagong Hill Tracts (CHT) Land Dispute Resolution Commission Act, which may allow for land restitution for indigenous people living in the CHT (see section 2.d).

f. Arbitrary or Unlawful Interference with Privacy, Family, Home, or Correspondence

The law does not prohibit arbitrary interference with private correspondence. Intelligence and law enforcement agencies may monitor private communications with the permission of MOHA. In practice, police rarely obtained warrants from the courts to monitor private correspondence, and authorities did not punish officers who violated these procedures. Human rights organizations alleged the Special Branch of police, the National Security Intelligence, and the Directorate General of Forces Intelligence employed informers to conduct surveillance and report on citizens perceived to be critical of the government. The Bangladesh Telecommunication Regulatory Commission (BTRC) tracked online content through its monitoring unit, and on November 6 it announced a decision to require internet cafes to install CCTV cameras to prevent "offensive content" from being uploaded. The government also routinely conducted surveillance on opposition politicians. Human rights organizations and news outlets reported police sometimes entered private homes without judicial or other appropriate authorization.

Section 2. Respect for Civil Liberties, Including:

a. Freedom of Speech and Press

The constitution provides for freedom of speech and press, but the government sometimes failed to respect these rights. There were significant limitations on freedom of speech. Some journalists self-censored their criticisms of the government due to harassment and fear of reprisal.

Freedom of Speech and Expression: The constitution equates criticism of the constitution with sedition. Punishment for sedition ranges from three years' to life imprisonment. Several high profile individuals were charged with sedition, including BNP leader Khaleda Zia, TV personality Mahmudur Rahman Manna, and reporter Kanok Sarwar, but the government did not proceed with prosecutions. The law limits hate speech but does not define clearly what constitutes hate speech, leaving the government with broad powers of interpretation. The government may restrict speech deemed to be against the security of the state; against friendly relations with foreign states; and against public order, decency, or morality; or that constitutes contempt of court, defamation, or incitement to an offense.

Press and Media Freedoms: Both print and online independent media were active and expressed a wide variety of views; however, media outlets that criticized the government experienced negative government pressure. For example, independent journalists alleged that intelligence services influenced media outlets in part by withholding financially important government advertising and pressing private companies to withhold their advertising as well.

The government maintains editorial control over the Bangladesh public television station (BTV), and private channels were mandated to air government content at no cost. Civil society said that there was political interference in the licensing process, as all television channel licenses granted by the government were for stations supporting the ruling party.

<u>Violence and Harassment</u>: Authorities, including intelligence services on some occasions, subjected journalists to physical attack, harassment, and intimidation. In February, members of the ruling party initiated 79 sedition and defamation cases in multiple courts against Mahfuz Anam, editor of *The Daily Star*, for publishing reports of corruption involving Prime Minister Hasina in 2007 and 2008. Hasina publicly stated Anam's newspaper and its sister media outlet, *Prothom Alo*, would be punished for publishing the reports.

The government imprisoned several prominent editors affiliated with the BNP, including the arrest of 81-year-old journalist Shafiq Rehman in April on charges relating to his alleged role in a plot to cause harm to Hasina's son. On September 6, the Supreme Court granted him three-month conditional bail after four and a half months of detention. The government continued to pursue charges against the editor of *Amar Desh*, Mahmudur Rahman, whom police arrested in 2013 for publishing Skype conversations between the Chairman of the ICT and a private consultant on ICT cases. Although the High Court granted Rahman bail on September 8, the Appellate Court chamber judge stayed his bail until October 30, further prolonging his detention of nearly four years. Rahman was released on bail on November 23.

<u>Censorship or Content Restrictions</u>: Privately owned newspapers usually enjoyed broad freedom to carry diverse views. Political polarization and self-censorship in an atmosphere of fear remained a problem, however. The media generally favored one of the two major political parties. Ownership of the media is influenced by politics, and both the government and big businesses used advertising as a weapon to control the media.

The government sought to censor the media indirectly through threats and harassment. On multiple occasions, government officials asked privately owned television channels not to broadcast the opposition's activities and statements. One talk show host reported overt censorship from Directorate General of Forces Intelligence personnel, who intimidated and threatened the host and the channel until owners finally cancelled the program. When the host continued working on another program, he reported receiving word for word instructions from security forces for behavior on air and being subject to surveillance and death threats via text, letter, and voice messages. The host was ultimately forced to flee the country. The well regarded newspapers *Prothom Alo* and *Daily Star* were denied access to prime-ministerial events because they published reports critical of the government and prime minister.

Both the government and businesses used the threat of pulling advertising dollars to pressure the media to avoid unfavorable coverage.

According to some journalists and human rights NGOs, journalists engaged in self-censorship, particularly due to fear of security-force retribution. Although public criticism of the government was common and vocal, some media figures expressed fear of harassment by the government.

The government did not subject foreign publications and films to stringent review and censorship. Some international media outlets reported delays and difficulties in obtaining visas. One television producer reported that the government would only issue a visa if the government were allowed to review and approve their coverage. A government-managed film censorship board reviewed local and foreign films and had the authority to censor or ban films on the grounds of state security, law and order, religious sentiment, obscenity, foreign relations, defamation, or plagiarism, but it was less strict than in the past. In January the Bangladesh Censor Board upheld a ban on the movie "Rana Plaza," originally set to premier in September 2015. The film told the story of a garment factory worker's 17-day fight to survive under debris following the April 24, 2013 eponymous factory collapse. Video rental libraries and DVD shops stocked a wide variety of films, and government efforts to enforce censorship on rentals were sporadic and ineffective.

The government at times censored objectionable comments regarding national leaders. In April, the government refiled a criminal defamation complaint against news editor Probir Sikder for "tarnishing the image" of a minister.

<u>National Security</u>: In some cases, the government criticized media outlets for reporting that allegedly compromised national security. The prime minister and other government officials criticized local media for their live telecast of government counter terrorism efforts during the July 1 Holey Bakery terrorist attack and, following the incident, the government enacted a blanket ban on live television news coverage of terrorist attack and disaster rescue operations.

<u>Nongovernmental Impact</u>: Atheist, secular, and LGBTI writers and bloggers reported they continued to receive death threats from extremist organizations. Following his inclusion in a "hit list" of 34 individuals published online by Ansar al-Islam (a purported AQIS affiliate) in November 2015, one blogger reported frequent threats via Facebook messenger and persistent surveillance, including an incident in April when four masked individuals with weapons followed him before

being scared away by police. On April 7, blogger Najimuddin Samad was killed in Dhaka; investigation into the murder was ongoing.

A journalist at a prominent newspaper reported receiving frequent death threats since September 2015, including from persons claiming affiliation with Da'esh. The journalist reported receiving almost daily text messages with threats and passages from the Quran describing death, such as "consider doomsday as if tomorrow," and "all will see the Prophet at the graveyard." Several other outlets experienced similar threats, some of which culminated in bias-based murders.

Internet Freedom

There were isolated incidents of government restriction and disruption of access to the internet and censorship of online content. Approximately 14.4 percent of the population has access to the internet according to the International Telecommunication Union. The BTRC reported approximately 63.9 million internet subscriptions in July, including roughly 60 million mobile internet subscriptions (one individual may have more than one subscription). Virtual Private Networks (VPNs) and Voice Over Internet Protocol (VOIP) telephony were illegal, but the laws were rarely enforced against individuals.

There were several incidents of government interference in internet communications, filtering or blocking of access, restricting content, and censoring websites or other communications and internet services. Many websites were suspended or closed based on vague criteria, or with explicit reference to their pro-opposition content in violation of legal requirements. The BTRC is charged with the regulation of telecommunications. It carries out law enforcement and government requests to block content by ordering internet service providers to take action. In May the BTRC blocked encrypted communication applications Threema and Wickr as well as several blogs and Facebook posts it deemed to be crafted in "malice to Islam." The BTRC Chairman later stated that the BTRC only blocks websites or services upon the request of law enforcement or MOHA and does not take independent action to block any websites or services. In July, the BTRC carried out a directive of the Dhaka Metropolitan Police to block 30 websites and Facebook pages for allegedly inciting militancy or running anti-religion propaganda. On August 2, the BTRC initiated a temporary shutdown of internet and mobile telephone services in a section of Dhaka city. BTRC officials stated that the exercise, the first in a series of temporary shutdowns, was to test the agency's ability to restrict access to communications to protect public safety in the event of an emergency, such as a terror attack. On August 4, the BTRC carried out a directive to block 35 news websites that had published material critical of the government and current political leaders or were perceived to feature overt support for political opposition groups. Many of the sites remained blocked at the end of the year.

Facebook's "biannual government requests report" for January to June 2016 showed the government made nine requests for data pursuant to legal process regarding eight users or accounts and one emergency request for data regarding one user or account in that period. Facebook reported producing some data in response to one request pursuant to legal process and one emergency request. The 10 total requests for data regarding nine users or accounts made by the government in the first half of 2016 is a slight decrease from the 12 requests for data regarding 31 users or accounts made in second half of 2015. Facebook further reported that two pieces of content were restricted at the BTRC's request in the first half of 2016, due to alleged violation of local law regarding blasphemy and the Bangladesh Information and Communications Technology Act.

Google's biannual transparency report for July to December 2015 showed the government made two requests for removal of two YouTube videos in that period. One request was related to alleged defamation and the other was related to alleged copyright violation. Google, which owns YouTube, did not comply with either request. Twitter's biannual Transparency Report for January to June 2016 showed no requests for data or content removal from the government. In Twitter's July to December 2015 report, the government made 10 requests for account information regarding 25 accounts, all pursuant to emergency disclosure requests. Law enforcement officers may submit an emergency disclosure request to Twitter on the basis of an exigent emergency that involves the danger of death or serious physical injury to a person that Twitter may have information necessary to protect. Twitter provided some information in response to six of those requests.

Individuals and groups generally engaged in the expression of views via the internet, although some activists stated that fear of prosecution under the Information and Communication Technology Act (ICTA) limited their online speech. The government used the ICTA and the threat of sedition charges, which carry a possible death penalty, to limit online activity and curtail freedom of expression online. The Bangladesh Telecommunication Regulatory Commission filtered internet content that the government deemed harmful to national unity and religious beliefs. The ICTA was amended in 2013 to increase penalties for cybercrime, make more offenses ineligible for bail, and give law enforcement officers broader authority to arrest violators without a court order. Opponents of the ICTA stated that section 57, which criminalizes the posting online of inflammatory or derogatory information against the state or individuals, stifles freedom of speech and is unconstitutional. The High Court previously rejected pleas challenging the constitutionality of section 57. The Cabinet approved a draft of the controversial digital security act in August, which includes a provision for life imprisonment for spreading negative propaganda through digital devices regarding the country's independence war and founding leader. The law was under review by the Law Ministry at the year's end.

Academic Freedom and Cultural Events

Although the government placed few restrictions on academic freedom or cultural events, media groups reported authorities discouraged research on sensitive religious and political topics that might fuel possible religious or communal tensions. Academic publications on the 1971 independence war were also subject to scrutiny and government approval. Appointment of teachers in universities continued to be politicized, and in September the Ministry of Education suggested that police or intelligence agencies should review teachers' personal information to ensure that they are not involved in antigovernment or criminal activities.

b. Freedom of Peaceful Assembly and Association

The constitution provides for the freedoms of assembly and association, but the government did not respect these rights for opposition political parties. The government limited both freedom of assembly and association for political reasons, ostensibly in the interest of national security.

Freedom of Assembly

The government generally permitted rallies of nonpolitical entities and its political allies, but on occasion, it prevented political opposition groups from holding meetings and demonstrations. The law authorizes the government to ban assemblies of more than four persons. A Dhaka Metropolitan Police order requires advance permission for gatherings such as protests and demonstrations. According to human rights NGOs, authorities increasingly used this provision, and preemptively banned gatherings around the election anniversary. Occasionally, police or ruling party activists used force to disperse demonstrations.

On April 4, police fired upon a crowd after an alleged attack by demonstrators gathered to protest the planned construction of a coal-fired power plant to

Chittagong District, killing four villagers and injuring 60. Following the protest, local authorities filed a legal case against 6,000 protesters for attacking the police and obstruction of law enforcers. The government, including the prime minister, supported construction of the power plant despite local concerns regarding economic and environmental impacts to the region. On July 28, police in Dhaka dispersed a march toward the prime minister's office to protest similarly the planned Rampal power plant near the ecologically sensitive Sunderbans. Police used tear gas and batons, injuring more than 50 individuals.

Police prevented opposition party members from holding events in several cases. For example, police allegedly stopped BNP rallies on July 27 in four sub-districts of Narayanganj, which were organized to protest the sentencing of BNP's senior vice chairman, Tarique Rahman, on corruption charges. Police prevented another BNP rally on October 2 to protest a government action against a BNP leader despite having given initial permission for the event.

Freedom of Association

The law provides for the right of citizens to form associations, subject to "reasonable restrictions" in the interest of morality or public order, and the government generally respected this right. The government's NGO Affairs Bureau sometimes withheld its approval for foreign funding to NGOs working in areas the bureau deemed sensitive such as human rights, labor rights, indigenous rights, or humanitarian assistance to Rohingya refugees (see sections 2.d., 5, and 7.a.).

On October 5, Parliament passed the Foreign Donations (Voluntary Activities) Regulation Act, which places additional restrictions on the receipt of foreign funds by NGOs or government officials and provides for punishment of NGOs making any 'derogatory' comments regarding the constitution or constitutional institutions (see section 5).

c. Freedom of Religion

See the Department of State's *International Religious Freedom Report* at www.state.gov/religiousfreedomreport/.

d. Freedom of Movement, Internally Displaced Persons, Protection of Refugees, and Stateless Persons

The law provides for freedom of movement within the country, foreign travel, emigration, and repatriation, and the government generally respected these rights, except in two sensitive areas--the CHT and Cox's Bazar. The government enforced some restrictions on foreigners' access to the CHT.

Abuse of Migrants, Refugees, and Stateless Persons: UNHCR reported cases of refugee abuse, including rape, assault, and domestic violence, deprivation of food, arbitrary detention, and documentation problems. From January to September, UNHCR reported a total of 168 cases of sexual and gender-based violence in the two official camps, including 129 cases of domestic violence and 14 cases of rape. According to a June IOM report, 53.5 percent of those surveyed in Rohingya populations living in makeshift settlements also experienced violence. Of those, 50.5 percent said they experienced physical violence, 6.5 percent said they experienced sexual violence, 3.8 percent said they experienced mental abuse, and 2.8 percent said they experienced food deprivation. These reports continued at year's end.

The government did not fully cooperate with the UN High Commissioner for Refugees (UNHCR) or other humanitarian organizations in providing protection and assistance to refugees, asylum seekers, stateless persons, and other persons of concern. For example, the government did not allow UNHCR access to all individuals whom UNHCR deemed persons of concern, particularly the undocumented Rohingya population living in the towns and villages outside of the two official refugee camps in Cox's Bazar district. UNHCR was also not allowed unrestricted access to a new influx of Rohingya migrants during the last three months of the year although the International Organization for Migration (IOM) was allowed to provide services.

Foreign Travel: Some senior opposition officials reported extensive delays in getting their passports renewed; others reported harassment and delays at the airport when departing the country. Authorities barred one BNP official from leaving the country to attend a party event in Bahrain while another was detained at the airport before being allowed to board a plane. Another opposition leader required High Court intervention in order to obtain his passport from the government after nearly a year of delays.

The international travel ban continued on war-crimes suspects from the 1971 independence war.

The country's passports are invalid for travel to Israel according to Bangladesh policy.

Internally Displaced Persons

Societal tensions and marginalization of indigenous people continued in the CHT as a result of a government policy during the 1973-1997 low-level armed conflict there of relocating landless Bengalis from the plains to the CHT with the unstated objective of changing the demographic balance in the CHT toward a Bengali majority, which displaced tens of thousands of indigenous persons.

The internally displaced persons (IDPs) in the CHT had limited physical security. Indigenous community leaders maintained that settlers' violations of indigenous persons' rights, sometimes with the involvement of security forces, were widespread.

The IDPs in the CHT also lacked sufficient access to courts and legal aid. The CHT Commission composed of experts from inside and outside the country, who sought to promote respect for rights in the CHT, found that a lack of information and lawyers to assist indigenous persons hindered IDP access to justice. The commission reported settlers expropriated indigenous land using false titles, intimidation, force, fraud, and manipulation of government eminent-domain claims (see section 6).

In August the government amended the Chittagong Hill Tracts (CHT) Land Dispute Resolution Commission Act curtailing the unilateral authority of the commission chair to make decisions on behalf of the commission and harmonizing the provisions with the CHT Peace Accord signed between the government and the Parbatya Chattagram Jana Samhati Samiti (PCJSS), a political party representing indigenous and tribal people of the CHT. Some Bengali groups, however, observed general strikes in CHT to protest the amendment, saying that it failed to recognize their rights as citizens of the country. They demanded inclusion of their representatives in the commission.

The number of IDPs in the CHT remained disputed. In 2000, a government task force estimated the number to be 500,000, which included nonindigenous as well as indigenous persons. The CHT Commission estimated that there were slightly more than 90,000 indigenous IDPs. The prime minister pledged to resolve outstanding land disputes in the CHT to facilitate the return of the IDPs and to close the remaining military camps, but the task force on IDPs remained unable to function due to a dispute over classifying settlers as IDPs. The commission reported that authorities displaced several indigenous families to create border guard camps and army recreational facilities. No land disputes were resolved during the year.

Protection of Refugees

As of August, the government and UNHCR provided temporary protection and basic assistance to 32,967 registered Rohingya refugees from Burma living in two official camps (Kutupalong and Nayapara). The government and UNHCR estimated that an additional 200,000 to 500,000 undocumented Rohingya lived in various villages and towns outside the two official refugee camps. Most of these undocumented Rohingya lived at unofficial sites among the local population in Teknaf and Ukhyia subdistricts of Cox's Bazar District. These sites included approximately 35,000 at the Kutupalong Makeshift site adjacent to the official Kutupalong refugee camp, 15,000 at a site called Leda, and 10,000 at the Shamlapur site. Starting in October, a new wave of more than 34,000 migrants entered Bangladesh, seeking refuge from violence in Rakhine state. Led by the Ministry of Foreign Affairs, the government continued to implement a national strategy on Rohingya with six key elements: border management, addressing security threats, humanitarian assistance, strengthened engagement with Burma, internal coordination on Rohingya problems, and surveying the undocumented Rohingya.

Starting in May, the government funded and implemented a survey of the undocumented Rohingya population in the six districts where they are most populous. As part of an awareness-raising campaign, the government stated that the survey would be used to improve services available to the undocumented Rohingya population. Other key messages of the awareness-raising campaign included that the survey was voluntary, would not lead to refugee status, and would not be used to force repatriation. Some NGOs and donor countries expressed concerns regarding how the survey will affect some portions of the undocumented Rohingya population, particularly children with one Bangladeshi and one Rohingya parent. The government stated its intent to issue "information cards" to those enumerated through the process, which can be used as proof of identity to authorities.

Access to Asylum: The law does not provide for granting asylum or refugee status, nor has the government established a formal system for providing protection to refugees. The government provided some protection to Rohingya refugees from

Burma already resident in the country, but it continued to deny asylum to the undocumented Rohingya, whom it categorized as illegal economic migrants. The government cooperated with UNHCR in providing temporary protection and basic assistance to registered refugees already resident in two official camps. Although significant protection problems remained, delivery of humanitarian assistance to the undocumented Rohingya has continued through implementation of the national strategy.

Refoulement: Continued violence and human rights abuses against the Rohingya in Burma prevented them from safely and voluntarily returning to their homes. Between January and September, according to UNHCR, Bangladeshi authorities forcibly turned back an estimated 3,487 Rohingya to Burma, compared with 4,719 during the same period in 2015. According to UNHCR, which maintained a field presence in both countries, many of these individuals were likely entitled to refugee status and protection. Despite these expulsions, the border remained porous, and UNHCR noted the existence of considerable daily cross-border movement for trade, smuggling, and illegal migration. The government of Bangladesh, including Prime Minister Hasina, engaged Burmese leader Aung San Suu Kyi regarding a durable solution to the Rohingya issue although these diplomatic efforts have not resulted in increased cooperation.

Freedom of movement: There were restrictions on refugees' freedom of movement. By law, refugees are not permitted to move outside of the two camps. Police can punish with detention any movement without valid documentation, including illegal entry and departure from the country.

Employment: The government did not authorize Rohingya refugees living in the country to work locally. Despite their movement restrictions, some refugees worked illegally as manual laborers or rickshaw pullers in the informal economy. Undocumented Rohingya also worked illegally, mostly in day-labor jobs.

Access to Basic Services: Working with UNHCR, the government continued to improve some aspects of the official refugee camps following findings in recent years that sanitation, nutrition, and shelter conditions had fallen below minimum international standards. Some basic needs remained unmet, and the camps remained overcrowded, with densities on par with the country's urban slums. A 2014 nutrition survey report from UNHCR and World Food Program stated the prevalence of malnourished (stunted) and underweight children in refugee camps remained higher than in the rest of the country and above the emergency threshold levels set by the World Health Organization.

Public education, while mandatory as of 2010 through eighth grade throughout the country, was offered only through seventh grade in the camps, compared with fifth grade in previous years. The government agreed to allow international NGOs to provide Rohingya outside the camps with access to informal education, starting with a group of 10,000 students. Government authorities did not allow refugees outside the camps to attend school, but some did so.

Government authorities did not allow registered or unregistered Rohingya formal and regular access to public health care. Instead, UNHCR and NGOs provided basic health services in the official camps to registered refugees, and IOM provided health services to the unregistered Rohingya in the makeshift sites. Although NGOs provided humanitarian assistance to registered Rohingya refugees, undocumented Rohingya, and the local population, the government's restrictions on NGO activities outside the camps limited the unregistered population's access to basic medical care and other services.

Four international NGOs provided basic services to undocumented Rohingya and to surrounding impoverished host communities. As with other NGOs, these organizations faced challenges working with the NGO Affairs Bureau. Some reported delays as long as three or four months in obtaining necessary permits for working with the Rohingya, which required coordinating with government officials at the local and national level.

Registered refugees did not have access to the formal legal system although they were able to take legal complaints to a local camp official who could mediate disputes. Members of the unregistered population had no legal protection and were sometimes arrested because the government viewed them as illegal economic migrants. Rohingya were sometimes harassed by security forces due to a perception among some groups, including the government, as well as members of indigenous groups in the CHT, that the Rohingya were responsible for perpetrating a range of criminal and terrorist activities in Southeastern Bangladesh, including through the Rohingya Solidarity Organization (RSO). For example, following the May 13 attack on security forces near the Nayapara official camp, authorities responded by detaining and questioning five Rohingya refugees, including an NGO volunteer.

Stateless Persons

The Rohingya in Bangladesh are legally stateless. Government and UNHCR estimates indicate that between 200,000 and 500,000 undocumented Rohingya are present in Bangladesh. They cannot derive citizenship from birth in the country, marriage with local citizens, or any other means.

Section 3. Freedom to Participate in the Political Process

The constitution provides citizens the ability to choose their government in free and fair periodic elections held by secret ballot and based on universal and equal suffrage, but recent elections were marred by government tampering and violence. Government restriction on freedom of expression and freedom of assembly limited the ability of opposition party members to participate effectively in the democratic process.

Elections and Political Participation

Recent Elections: BNP, the main opposition party, boycotted the January 2014 parliamentary elections, leaving more than half of all seats uncontested and many more only nominally contested, thereby decreasing the people's access to meaningful electoral choice. Prime Minister Hasina and the ruling AL party retained power with 235 of 300 elected seats. After its boycott of the elections, the BNP held no seats in parliament. The official opposition party, the Jatiya Party, which had 36 elected seats, was also part of the ruling coalition. Parties that supported the government held most of the remaining seats. Sheikh Hasina's cabinet included representatives from the other parties in her coalition. Most international observers regarded these elections as flawed.

During the year, in six rounds of union council elections in May and June, more than 126 people were killed and approximately 9,000 were injured as a result of electoral violence. Opposition parties and independent observers repeatedly challenged the credibility of the Election Commission. In October, the general secretary of the AL rejected the prospect of dialogue with the BNP on creation of an independent election commission. On November 29, the Election Commission publicly apologized to the high court for not investigating any of the grievances associated with this year's local elections, demonstrating a pronounced lack of independence.

Political Parties and Political Participation: The government mobilized law enforcement resources to level civil and criminal charges against opposition party leaders, including BNP leader Khaleda Zia and Senior Vice Chairman Tarique

Rahman. Jamaat leaders could not operate openly, as they were harassed by law enforcement and were blamed by the AL for the recent increase in terrorism. Media outlets critical of the government and AL were subject to government intimidation, lawsuits, and forced closure. AL-affiliated organizations (such as the student wing) reportedly carried out violence and intimidation around the country, including against individuals affiliated with opposition groups.

In some instances the government interfered with the right of opposition parties to organize public functions and restricted the broadcasting of opposition political events. Jamaat's appeal of a 2012 Supreme Court decision cancelling the party's registration continued in the midst of new draft legislation banning any organization found guilty of war crimes, pending at year's end.

Participation of Women and Minorities: There is no provision to reserve parliamentary seats for minorities. Women have 50 reserved parliamentary seats out of a total of 350. Those who hold the 50 seats are appointed by the parties rather than directly elected by constituents.

Section 4. Corruption and Lack of Transparency in Government

The law provides criminal penalties for corruption by officials, but the government did not implement the law effectively. Officials frequently engaged in corrupt practices with impunity. Human rights groups, the media, the Anticorruption Commission (ACC), and other institutions reported government corruption.

Corruption remained a serious problem within the judiciary and was a factor in lengthy delays of trials, which facilitated witness tampering and intimidation of victims. Several reports by human rights groups and corruption watchdog groups indicated continued public dissatisfaction with the perceived politicization of the judiciary. The government subjected the judiciary to political pressure (see section 1.e.), and cases involving opposition leaders often proceeded in an irregular fashion.

Corruption: Some in civil society stated the government was not serious about fighting corruption and that it used the ACC for politically motivated prosecutions. A 2013 amendment to the ACC Law removed the ACC's authority to sue public servants without prior government permission. The ACC reported that the defendant was convicted in 32 percent of adjudicated cases, which is an increase of 10 percent from last year. The court started to pursue some cases against lower-level government officials and some higher-level officials. A large backlog of cases remains, however. As of November, the ACC filed 266 new graft cases in addition to the 3,097 cases that were pending at the end of 2015.

The ACC continued to pursue a case filed in 2007 against Housing and Public Works Minister Mosharraf Hossain for amassing illegal wealth worth 30 million taka ($383,000). In July, the High Court allowed the ACC to continue investigation of the case and directed Mosharraf to surrender to a lower court. In October, Mosharraf told media that the ACC would face trouble if it continued to investigate two senior officials in the Capital Development Authority for misappropriation of funds. The ACC also continued its case against MP Abdur Rahman Bodi from Cox's Bazar, who was released on bail, for amassing illegal wealth. Bodi was implicated in at least 23 cases, including human trafficking and drug smuggling, and was present during a meeting between alleged terrorists and a Saudi national that was disrupted by the Bangladesh Border Guard in July. On November 2, a Dhaka court convicted Bodi of concealment of wealth and sentenced him to two years in prison, fined him one million taka and sent him to jail. Bodi, however, filed an appeal with the High Court, which released him on bail.

In some cases, the ACC was used by the government as a political tool. In July the High Court convicted Tarique Rahman, senior vice chairman of the BNP, of money laundering following the ACC's appeal of a lower court verdict acquitting him of charges. Rahman was sentenced to seven years in prison and fined 200 million taka (more than $2.5 million), and in November the High Court asked authorities to start trials for two tax evasion and three extortion cases against him from 2007 and 2008.

The government took steps to address widespread police corruption. The IGP continued to train police to address corruption and create a more responsive police force. A current year report from the Asia Foundation found that public trust in the police was lower than any other public institution with 45 percent of respondents believing them to have low or very low integrity.

According to a June report from Transparency International Bangladesh (TIB), 58 percent of households surveyed paid a bribe in 2015, amounting to more than 88 trillion taka ($1.1 billion) of bribes paid in the service sector. The NGO asserted that the highest levels of graft were related to passport services, law enforcement, education, the road transport authority, and the land administration.

<u>Financial Disclosure</u>: The law requires candidates for parliament file statements of personal wealth with the Election Commission. The ACC has responsibility for investigating related complaints to illegally gained wealth, but it dropped investigations of some politicians for amassing wealth unexplained by known sources of income after the politicians stated they made mistakes on their wealth affidavits.

<u>Public Access to Information</u>: The law provides for public access to government information, but it was not effective. The Information Commission is responsible for implementing the law, which lists a few exceptions (e.g., national security) and establishes nominal processing fees. The commission has the authority to issue summonses compelling individuals who do not comply with a request for information to give oral or written evidence under oath. Observers noted that the commission filed few cases during the year due to citizens' limited understanding of the law and limited capacity to file and pursue requests for information. The commission conducted public outreach and training of public officials to encourage effective use of the law.

Section 5. Governmental Attitude Regarding International and Nongovernmental Investigation of Alleged Violations of Human Rights

A wide variety of domestic and international human rights groups generally operated independently, investigating and publishing their findings on human rights cases. Although human rights groups often sharply criticized the government, they also practiced some self-censorship. Observers noted that a "culture of fear" had diminished the strength of civil society, exacerbated by threats from extremists and an increasingly entrenched leading political party. Even civil society members affiliated with the ruling party reported receiving threats of arrest from the security forces for their public criticism of government policies.

The government continued to restrict the funding and operations of the human rights organization Odhikar since the 2013 publication of an Odhikar report that many independent observers believed significantly exaggerated the government's use of force during a Hefazat-e-Islam rally. The report included a count of resulting deaths that differed considerably from the official number and other independent estimates. Although the ACC dropped its case against Odhikar in June, Odhikar representatives continued to report harassment by government officials and security forces, including disruption of their planned events. Odhikar reported investigations into its finances that it regarded as harassment and the blockage by the NGO Affairs Bureau of foreign funds, including a grant from the European Union. Family members and Odhikar staff reported additional harassment and claimed their telephone calls, e-mails, and movements were under constant surveillance by security officers.

The government required all NGOs, including religious organizations, to register with the Ministry of Social Welfare. Local and international NGOs working on sensitive topics or groups, such as religious issues, human rights, indigenous people, LGBTI communities, Rohingya refugees, or worker rights, faced both formal and informal governmental restrictions. In July, the State Minister for Social Welfare Nuruzzaman Ahmed told parliament that his ministry would investigate and cancel the registration for any NGO involved in "anti-state activities." International NGOs that assist Rohingya refugees and work with organized labor reported difficulties in meeting stringent government administrative requirements. Some of these groups claimed intelligence agencies monitored them. The government sometimes restricted international NGOs' ability to operate through delays in project registration, cease-and-desist letters, and visa refusals. Some civil society members reported repeated audits by the National Board of Revenue. The government countered NGO criticism through the media, sometimes with intimidating or threatening remarks, and through the courts (see section 1.e.). In October, NGOs discovered that the NGO Affairs Bureau posted on its public website detailed information for foreigners employed by NGOs in the country, including names, passport numbers, local addresses, e-mail addresses, and local telephone numbers, creating a significant security risk.

Following a two-year drafting process, parliament passed the Foreign Donations (Voluntary Activities) Regulation Act on October 5, placing stricter control over the foreign funding of NGOs and enacting punitive provisions for those NGOs that make "derogatory" comments regarding the constitution of the country, its founding history, or constitutional bodies (i.e., government institutions and leaders). NGO leaders stated that the bill infringes on their constitutional right to freedom of expression, to which prominent MP Suranjit Sengupta responded that NGOs are not entitled to freedom of expression. NGOs also stated that the law was unclear, autocratic, subject to interpretation, and contrary to the constitution.

The law also includes a provision that will require NGOs to obtain preauthorization for obtaining funds from foreign individuals, and for NGOs' sub-grantees to do the same, which will negatively affect the ability of some organizations to operate. The bill will also require approval and monitoring of each project by the NGO Affairs Bureau and give the director general of the bureau the authority to impose sanctions, including fines up to three times the amount of the foreign donation or closure of an NGO. Some NGOs reported that the NGO Affairs Bureau had pushed them toward service delivery and away from rights-based awareness raising or NGO capacity building.

Government Human Rights Bodies: The NHRC has seven members, including five honorary positions. Observers noted that the NHRC's small government support staff was inadequate and underfunded. The NHRC's primary activity was educating the public about human rights and ostensibly advising the government on key human rights issues. The International Coordinating Committee of National Institutions for the Promotion and Protection of Human Rights found that the NHRC did not fully comply with international standards for such bodies. Specifically, the coordinating committee focused on the lack of transparency in selecting NHRC commissioners and the NHRC's lack of hiring authority over its support staff. In August, the government appointed Kazi Rezaul Haque as the new chairman of the NHRC through a process that lacked transparency and limited civil society participation.

Section 6. Discrimination, Societal Abuses, and Trafficking in Persons

Women

The law specifically prohibits certain forms of discrimination against women, provides special procedures for prosecuting persons accused of violence against women and children, calls for harsh penalties for these offenses, provides compensation to victims, and requires action against investigating officers for negligence or willful failure of duty. Enforcement was weak. Laws regarding marriage, divorce, custody, and inheritance differed according to an individual's religion and were often discriminatory toward women and girls.

Rape and Domestic Violence: The law prohibits rape and physical spousal abuse, but it does not criminalize marital rape. Rape can be punished by life imprisonment or the death penalty. Gender-based violence remained a serious challenge. The Bangladesh Bureau of Statistics (BBS) *Report on Violence Against Women Survey 2015* released in October found that 80.2 percent of women were abused by a husband or male partner at least once in their lifetime, a finding lower than the 2011 survey in which 87.1 percent of women reported abuse. While the government operated a confidential helpline for reporting abuse, nationally only 2.4 percent of women and girls knew about it and only 2.6 percent took legal action according to the survey. Human rights organization Ain O Shalish Kendro

(ASK) documented 101 killings of women by their husbands between January and June. Of the 442 rape cases recorded from January to August, 107 victims were between the ages of seven and 12 years of age. Twenty-three victims were killed after being raped, and six rape victims committed suicide. Admissions to treatment centers for victims of GBV indicated a 10 percent increase in rape and other violence against women in the third quarter of the year.

According to human rights monitors, many victims did not report rapes due to lack of access to legal services, social stigma, or fear of further harassment and the legal requirement to furnish witnesses. As a result, the prosecution of rapists was weak and inconsistent. Media reported that between 2001 and 2015, 22,386 women and children received treatment for rape and other violence at the government-run One Stop Crisis Centers located at 10 government hospitals. Of these, 5,003 cases were filed, resulting in 820 verdicts, and punishment for only 101 perpetrators.

A 2013 UN multiagency study on violence against women surveyed almost 2,400 men between the ages of 18 and 49 in one urban and one rural area of the country. According to the study, 55 percent of urban male respondents and 57 percent of rural respondents reported they themselves had perpetrated physical and/or sexual violence against women. The study concluded that the low prosecution rate of rapists supported a culture of impunity and encouraged further criminal acts by respondents who admitted to perpetrating rape. In total, 88 percent of rural respondents and 95 percent of urban respondents reported they faced no legal consequences for rape charges.

In October, 23-year-old Khadiza Begum Nargis, a student at Sylhet Government Women's College, was hacked repeatedly on her head with a machete by Badrul Alam, a fourth-year student at Shahjalal University of Science and Technology (SUST) and the senior assistant secretary of SUST's Bangladesh Chatra League unit. The attack was carried out on the campus of Murari Chand College where the victim had gone to take an exam. The attack was partially videotaped by a bystander with a mobile phone, and the clip went viral on social media, prompting outrage. While it appears that no one intervened during the attack, according to media reports, some bystanders chased Badrul when he tried to flee following the assault. Badrul confessed to hacking Khadiza with the intent to kill her after she refused his advances. Murari Chand College students formed a human-chain to protest the killing, while others took to Facebook and other social media platforms to vent their anger at the brutality of the attack and demand justice for Khadiza. The SUST administration expelled Badrul and formed a three-member committee to probe the incident. Badrul is in police custody and his trial was ongoing in

December. Nargis survived the attack after emerging from a coma and continued to receive medical treatment at the end of the year.

The government operated a confidential hotline and 68 hospital-based crisis centers for survivors of domestic violence at the divisional, district, and sub-district levels where domestic violence survivors receive health care, police assistance, legal advice, and psychosocial counseling. There were some support groups for survivors of domestic violence. The number and capacity of legal aid services and shelter homes were inadequate compared to the need and were unsustainable given their reliance on project funding, according to the September Citizens' Initiatives on the Convention for the Elimination of All Forms of Discrimination Against Women--Bangladesh (CIC-BD) Alternative Report.

In August, following advocacy by Bangladesh Legal Aid and Services Trust (BLAST) and other human rights groups, the High Court Division of the Supreme Court directed forensics experts to submit their opinions on the so-called "two-finger" rape test. During the test, a doctor assesses whether a woman has had sexual intercourse by inserting two fingers into her vagina to determine her "vaginal laxity" by checking for presence of the hymen. Human rights organizations and the broader medical community contend that the test is unscientific, has no forensic value, and retraumatizes survivors. Human rights organizations viewed the directive as a sign of progress toward ending the practice. Despite recent development of The National Action Plan to Prevent Violence Against Women and Girls (2013-2025), human rights monitors, including CIC-BD, noted concern about the plan's limited focus on prevention and resource allocation. In consultation with NGOs, the government established a committee to implement the plan.

Other Harmful Traditional Practices: Some NGOs reported violence against women related to disputes over dowries. In a current year report, the organization Bangladesh Mahila Parishad documented 302 women who were tortured due to dowry issues in the first nine months of 2015 and another 161 who were killed. In July, media reported that a husband beat his wife because he received a dowry of 80,000 taka ($1,016) and not the 100,000 taka ($1,270) that he had demanded. Police later arrested the man, and there was no further information about the outcome of the arrest at year's end.

A Supreme Court Appellate Division ruling allows the use of fatwas (religious edicts) only to settle religious matters; fatwas may not be invoked to justify punishment, nor may they supersede secular law. Islamic tradition dictates that only those religious scholars with expertise in Islamic law may declare a fatwa. Despite these restrictions, village religious leaders sometimes made such declarations. The declarations resulted in extrajudicial punishments, often against women, for perceived moral transgressions. In August, following advocacy from BLAST, the Ministry of Local Government, Rural Development, and Cooperatives ordered district commissioners to mandate local councils to prevent extrajudicial punishments in their areas.

Incidents of vigilantism against women occurred, sometimes led by religious leaders enforcing fatwas. The incidents included whipping, beating, and other forms of physical violence. In August, media reported that a local council member in Rangpur named Aktar Hossain directed that a local woman and man be punished for an "extramarital affair" that occurred when the man broke into the woman's house while her husband was gone. Without hearing testimony from the woman, the council member determined that she be caned 101 times by her husband before 400 assembled villagers while the council member caned the man 20 times.

Acid attacks, although less common than in the past, remained a serious problem. Assailants threw acid in the faces of victims--usually women--leaving them disfigured and often blind. Acid attacks were often related to a woman's refusal to accept a marriage proposal or in connection with land disputes. A prominent local NGO reported 36 acid attacks harming 42 victims from January through September. In January, a court in Sylhet sentenced Muhammed Laike Ahmed to 14 years in prison for throwing acid on a teenage girl in 2012 after she spurned his numerous proposals.

The law seeks to control the availability of acid and reduce acid-related violence directed toward women, but lack of awareness of the law and poor enforcement limited its effect. The Commerce Ministry restricted acid sales to buyers registered with relevant trade organizations; however, the government did not enforce the restrictions universally. To facilitate speedier prosecution of acid-throwing cases, the law provides special tribunals and generally does not allow bail. According to the Acid Survivors Foundation, the special tribunals were not effective, and conviction rates remained low.

Sexual Harassment: Sexual harassment in public and private, including in educational institutions and workplaces, is prohibited by a 2009 High Court guideline. The Bangladesh National Woman Lawyers' Association noted in June that harassment remained a problem and monitoring and enforcement of the guidelines were poor, which sometimes prevented girls from attending school or work. The formation of complaints committees and the installation of complaints boxes at educational institutions and workplaces required by the Court's directive were rarely enforced, according to the CIC-BD Alternative Report. Between January and June, ASK documented 148 cases of sexual harassment against women with three victims committing suicide. According to NGOs and media reports, cyber sexual harassment is also a growing problem.

Reproductive Rights: Couples and individuals had the right to decide the number, spacing, and timing of their children; to manage their reproductive health; and to have access to the information and means to do so, free from discrimination, coercion, or violence. Civil society organizations, however, reported that victims of child marriage often lacked the means to access services. According to the 2014 Bangladesh Demographic and Health Survey (BDHS), the total fertility rate for women aged 15 to 49 was 2.3 children per woman, and 62.4 percent of married women used any method of contraception (54.1 percent used any modern method); 12.1 percent of women had unmet family planning needs. Weaknesses in the public health system, such as lack of trained providers and equipment in hard-to-reach and hard-to-staff areas, resulted in inequitable access to information and services around the country. A full range of contraceptive methods, including long-acting reversible contraception and permanent methods, were available through government, NGO and for-profit clinics and hospitals. Pharmacies and social marketing kiosks carried a wide range of family planning options and sold 41 percent of the family planning supplies distributed in the country, according to the 2014 BDHS. Most low-income families relied on public family planning services offered free of cost. The survey indicated that low levels of income and education, some religious beliefs, and traditional family roles sometimes served as barriers to access.

According to a 2015 estimate by the World Bank, during the preceding twenty-five years, maternal mortality ratio declined from 569 to 176 deaths per 100,000 live births.

Discrimination: The constitution declares all citizens equal before the law with entitlement to equal protection of the law. It also explicitly recognizes the equal rights of women "in all spheres of the state and of public life." Nevertheless, women do not enjoy the same legal status and rights as men in family, property, and inheritance law. Under traditional Islamic inheritance law, daughters inherit only half of what sons do. Under Hindu inheritance law, a widow's rights to her deceased husband's property are limited to her lifetime and revert to the male heirs upon her death.

Women faced sexual harassment at work, as well as difficulties in being promoted in factory jobs, obtaining access to credit, and other economic opportunities. The government's National Women's Development Policy included commitments to provide opportunities for women in employment and business.

Children

<u>Birth Registration</u>: The law does not grant citizenship automatically by birth within the country. Individuals become citizens if their fathers or grandfathers were born in the territories that are now part of the country. If a person qualifies for citizenship through ancestry, the father or grandfather must have been a permanent resident of these territories in or after 1971. Birth registration is required to obtain a national identity card or passport

<u>Education</u>: Primary education was free and compulsory through fifth grade, and the government offered subsidies to parents to keep girls in class through 10th grade. While teacher fees and uniforms remained prohibitively costly for many families, the government distributed hundreds of millions of free textbooks to increase access to education. Enrollments in primary schools showed gender parity, but educational attainment was low for both boys and girls. The completion rates fell in secondary school with more girls than boys at the secondary level. The 2010 Education Policy extended compulsory primary education to the eighth grade; however, in the absence of legal amendments to reflect the policy, it remained unenforceable. Government incentives to families who sent children to school contributed significantly to increased primary school enrollments in recent years, but hidden school fees at the local level created barriers to access for the poorest families, particularly for girls. Many families kept children out of school to become wage earners or to help with household chores, and primary school coverage was insufficient in hard-to-reach and disaster-prone areas. Early and forced marriage was a factor in girls' attrition from secondary school.

<u>Child Abuse</u>: Despite strong children's rights legislation, there was a general lack of enforcement due to limited resources and capacity to implement and monitor these laws. Governance remained weak with responsibility for children held by one of the least-resourced ministries, the Ministry of Women and Children's Affairs. Many forms of child abuse, including sexual abuse, physical and humiliating punishment, child abandonment, kidnapping, and trafficking, continued to be serious and widespread problems. Children were vulnerable to abuse in all settings: home, community, school, residential institutions, and the

workplace. In October, the government, with support from UNICEF, launched "Child Helpline--1098," a free telephone service designed to help children facing violence, abuse, and exploitation.

According to the ASK, 683 children were victims of violence from January to August, with 51 victims aged six or younger and 234 victims aged seven to 12 years old. One hundred seventy-three children were raped, 33 were sexually harassed by stalkers, 14 were tortured by law enforcement agencies, 277 were tortured by teachers, and 87 experienced other types of physical torture. This followed a year in which such cases increased 161 percent between 2014 and 2015. The Prime Minister expressed concern about the surge in child murders in her speech at the Parliament in February.

Girls were especially vulnerable to violence and abuse. Findings from the Bangladesh Bureau of Statistics' *Report on Violence Against Women Survey 2015* indicated that 34.2 percent of girls aged 10-14 years have been raped at least once. The rate is 39.7 percent for those aged 15-19 years. In August, Suraiya Akter Risha, a 14-year-old eighth grader at Willes Little Flower School in Dhaka, was attacked in broad daylight by a knife-wielding assailant as she was leaving the school premises. Her death three days later sparked protests by students, teachers, and parents.

Despite advances, including establishing a monitoring agency in the Ministry of Home Affairs, trafficking of children and inadequate care and protection for survivors of trafficking continued to be problems. Child labor and abuse at the workplace remained problems in certain industries, mostly in the informal sector, and child domestic workers were vulnerable to all forms of abuse at their informal workplaces (see section 7.c.).

Early and Forced Marriage: The legal age of marriage is 18 for women and 21 for men, according to the Child Marriage Restraint Act, 1929, but the law is poorly enforced, and early and forced marriage remained a serious problem. According to 2016 UNICEF data, 52 percent of girls were married by age 18, and 18 percent were married by age 15. The median age of first marriage and first sexual intercourse, according to the 2014 BDHS, was 15.8 and 15.9 years old, respectively.

The Bangladesh Government drafted a new Child Marriage Restraint Act in 2015, which was the subject of intense national debate. The Act increases penalties for those arranging underage marriages but drafts included a clause that will allow marriage of children below the age of 18 under special circumstances. Despite assurances from the Government of Bangladesh not to reduce the legal age of marriage under any circumstance in the wake of intense advocacy on the part of human rights advocates and development donors protesting the clause, the cabinet approved the draft law, which was pending with parliament at year's end. The Prime Minister publicly defended the draft act despite criticism from domestic sources and the international community. In an effort to reduce early and forced marriages, the government offered stipends for girls' school expenses beyond the compulsory fifth-grade level. The government and NGOs conducted workshops and public events to teach parents the importance of their daughters waiting until age 18 before marrying. The average age of marriage for females was less than 18, and as such children were among the victims of dowry and other marital violence.

Sexual Exploitation of Children: The penalty for sexual exploitation of children is 10 years' to life imprisonment. The 2013 Children's Act defines a child as anyone under age 18. Child pornography and the selling or distributing of such material is prohibited. The Pornography Control Act sets the maximum penalty at 10 years in prison and a fine of 500,000 taka ($6,250). In 2009, the most recent year for such data, the International Labor Organization (ILO) and BBS completed a baseline survey on commercial sexual exploitation of children. According to the survey, of 18,902 child victims of sexual exploitation, 83 percent were girls, nine percent were transgender children, and eight percent were boys. The survey reported that 40 percent of the girls and 53 percent of the boys were under age 16, the age of consent when the survey was conducted. The age of consent is 18 for women and 21 for men.

International Child Abductions: The country is not a party to the 1980 Hague Convention on the Civil Aspects of International Child Abduction. See the Department of State's *Annual Report on International Parental Child Abduction* at travel.state.gov/content/childabduction/en/legal/compliance.html.

Anti-Semitism

There was no Jewish community in the country, but politicians and imams reportedly used anti-Semitic statements to gain support from their constituencies. In one high profile case, ruling party politicians leveraged anti-Semitic sentiment for political gain by accusing an opposition leader of colluding with Israeli intelligence services.

Trafficking in Persons

See the State Department's *Trafficking in Persons Report* at
www.state.gov/j/tip/rls/tiprpt/.

Persons with Disabilities

The Rights and Protection of Persons with Disabilities Act, 2013 provides for equal treatment and freedom from discrimination for persons with disabilities; however, persons with disabilities faced social and economic discrimination. The law focuses on prevention of disability, treatment, education, rehabilitation, social protection, employment, transport accessibility, and advocacy.

The law requires persons with disabilities to register for identity cards to track their enrollment in educational institutions and access to jobs. It allows them to be included in voter lists, to cast votes, and to participate in elections. It states that no person, organization, authority, or corporation shall discriminate against persons with disabilities and allows for fines up to 500,000 taka ($6,250) or three years' imprisonment for giving unequal treatment for school, work, or inheritance based on disability, although implementation of the law is uneven. Support programs tended to push people living with disabilities toward vocational training instead of formal education. The law also created a 27-member National Coordination Committee charged with coordinating relevant activities among all government organizations and private bodies to fulfill the objectives of the law.

According to the Ministry of Public Administration, 1 percent of civil service first- and second-class jobs--gazette officers with more power and responsibilities than other classes--are reserved for persons with disabilities. According to the Center for Disability in Development, 148 union parishads (local government councils) have disability inclusion initiatives.

According to the NGO Action against Disability, 90 percent of children with disabilities did not attend public school. The government trained teachers about inclusive education and recruited disability specialists at the district level. The government also allocated stipends for students with disabilities.

The law contains extensive accessibility requirements for new buildings. Nevertheless, authorities approved construction plans for new buildings that did not meet these requirements.

The law affords persons with disabilities the same access to information rights as nondisabled persons, but family and community dynamics often influenced whether these rights were exercised. The law contains provisions for information and communications technology to be accessible to persons with disabilities through video subtitling, sign language, screen readers, or text-to-speech systems in public and private media outlets. The state television channel used sign language, but general practice by the media did not meet the requirements of the law.

The law identifies persons with disabilities as a priority group for government-sponsored legal services. The Ministry of Social Welfare, Department of Social Services, and National Foundation for the Development of the Disabled are the government agencies responsible for protecting the rights of persons with disabilities. Due to problems of accessibility and to discrimination, persons with disabilities were sometimes excluded from mainstream government health, education, and social protective services. The government reduced taxes on several hundred items, such as wheelchairs, hearing aids, Braille machines, orthotics, and prostheses, designed to assist persons with disabilities.

Government facilities for treating persons with mental disabilities were inadequate. The Ministry of Health established child development centers in all public medical colleges to assess neurological disabilities. Several private initiatives existed for medical and vocational rehabilitation as well as for employment of persons with disabilities. National and international NGOs provided services and advocated for persons with disabilities. The government established service centers for persons with disabilities in all 64 districts, where local authorities provided free rehabilitation services and assistive devices. The government also promoted autism research and awareness.

National/Racial/Ethnic Minorities

Violent attacks against religious minority communities continued, apparently motivated by transnational violent extremism as well as economic and political reasons. Attackers purporting to be affiliated with Da'esh and AQIS claimed to kill eight Hindus, two Christians, two Buddhists, as well as one Sufi and one Shi'a adherent. Four Hindus and two Buddhists were seriously injured in other attacks by religious extremists.

On October 30, 150-200 people vandalized 200 homes and at least five temples in the eastern Bangladesh subdistrict of Nasirnagar, reportedly injuring 150 people and setting fire to eight shops. The attack followed a Facebook post by a local resident showing a doctored photo with a Hindu deity pasted over the Kaaba in Mecca. A National Human Rights Commission fact-finding mission to the district reported on November 2 that the attacks were deliberate and aimed at driving out Hindus so as to grab their land. The Bangladesh Hindu Buddhist Christian Unity Council (BHBCUC) asserted that the local administration and the local Member of Parliament were responsible for failing to prevent the attacks. A police investigation found that a feud between ruling party members precipitated the attacks. Government officials, students, Hindu organizations, and others condemned the attacks, although there was disagreement on the cause. Police detained approximately 100 people, including the owner of the internet café where the photo was uploaded; many had tenuous links to the incident.

Religious minority advocacy groups, including the BHBCUC, criticized the government for not adequately protecting the country's religious minorities. In June, Hindu leaders decried attacks that disproportionately targeted Hindus, imploring Indian authorities to intervene.

Some members of religious minorities reported private discrimination in employment and housing. Urdu-speaking minority communities reported systemic discrimination, including lack of access to employment and land. Discrimination against minorities in land tenure, combined with the lack of witness protection, at times made it difficult to stem land grabbing and to prosecute detained suspects.

Minority communities reported many land ownership disputes that disproportionately displaced minorities, especially in areas near new roads or industrial development zones where land prices had recently increased. They also claimed that local police, civil authorities, and political leaders were sometimes involved or shielded politically influential land grabbers from prosecution (see section 6.). In August, the government amended the Chittagong Hill Tracts (CHT) Land Dispute Resolution Commission Act, which may allow for land restitution for indigenous people living in the CHT (see section 2.d).

NGOs reported that national origin, racial, and ethnic minorities faced discrimination. For example, some Dalits (lowest-caste Hindus) had restricted access to land, adequate housing, education, and employment.

Indigenous People

The indigenous community experienced widespread discrimination and abuse, despite government quotas for participation of indigenous CHT residents in the civil service and higher education, as well as provisions for local governance as called for in the 1997 CHT Peace Accord. Indigenous persons from the CHT were unable to participate effectively in decisions affecting their lands due to disagreements regarding the structure and policies of the land commission. Parbatya Chattagram Jana Samhati Samiti, a political party formed to represent the people and indigenous tribes of the CHT, alleged that the ruling party, with support from local administration and security forces, used violence, intimidation, and vote-rigging to establish control over the CHT during the local council elections in June. Strict security measures prevented some indigenous individuals and activists from combating discrimination.

Indigenous persons also suffered from societal violence, including rape and murder. This violence was sometimes associated with land grabbing. According to a current year report from the Kapaeeng Foundation, an indigenous rights NGO, in 2015 134 indigenous people, including 101 from the CHT, were physically assaulted by Bengali nonstate actors, complicit with law enforcement agencies. Kapaeeng reported that 85 indigenous women and girls were sexually or physically assaulted in 2015, including 26 cases of rape, and 13 indigenous people were killed. In 2015, 84 houses belonging to indigenous people were vandalized and 35 were burned to the ground.

The government recognized indigenous people living in the CHT as having special status, and the constitution allows for affirmative action in favor of indigenous people, but indigenous groups reported that effective affirmative action did not occur. Some NGOs reported discrimination against indigenous people in government hiring and promotions. According to the CHT Commission, fewer than half of indigenous children ages six through 10 were enrolled in school in part due to a lack of indigenous-language instruction. Indigenous people at times lacked access to adequate housing and health care.

Indigenous groups and NGOs reported monitoring by civilian and military intelligence agencies, especially in the CHT, which had a pronounced military presence.

The central government retained authority over land use. The land commission, designed to investigate and return all illegally acquired land, did not resolve any disputes as of October. Bengalis and indigenous persons questioned the structure and impartiality of the commission. An August amendment to the CHT Land

Dispute Resolution Commission Act was designed to address this issue, but it has been challenged by Bengali settlers to the area who feel it does not represent their interests (see section 2.d). Some indigenous people reporting losing land as a result of implementation of the recent Land Border Agreement with India.

Indigenous communities in areas other than the CHT reported the loss of land to Bengali Muslims, and indigenous peoples' advocacy groups reported continued land encroachment by Rohingya settlers from Burma. The government continued construction projects on land traditionally owned by indigenous communities in the Moulvibazar and Modhupur forest areas.

On November 6, members of the Santal community, a mostly Christian indigenous group which numbers approximately 500,000 in Bangladesh, clashed over land ownership with the workers of a sugar mill and police in the northern district of Gaibandha. According to media reports, three people were killed and 25 were injured in the clash during which Santal protesters fired bows and arrows at police who returned fire with teargas and rubber bullets. Police and ruling party activists evicted approximately 2,500 Santal families and looted and set fire to their houses during the incident. The conflict emerged when a hundred Santal protesters tried to reoccupy land the government had acquired in a 1952 agreement with their ancestors to grow sugarcane. Santal protesters claimed local authorities breached the agreement by leasing out part of the land for cultivation of crops other than sugarcane. On November 7, police filed criminal charges against 42 named and some 400 unnamed people for alleged involvement in the attack on the police. In December, video footage posted online of police seeing fire to Santal houses during the November 6 event sparked public outrage. Police stated that they were reviewing the evidence at the year's end.

Acts of Violence, Discrimination, and Other Abuses Based on Sexual Orientation and Gender Identity

Consensual same-sex sexual activity is illegal under Section 377 of the Code of Criminal Procedure, but the law was not enforced. LGBTI groups reported police used the law as a pretext to bully LGBTI individuals, including those considered effeminate regardless of their sexual orientation, as well as to limit registration of LGBTI organizations. Some groups also reported harassment under a suspicious behavior provision of the police code. The Hijra population has long been a marginalized, but recognized, part of society, but faced elevated levels of fear, harassment, and law enforcement contact in the wake of violent extremist attacks against vulnerable communities. The government acknowledged the existence of the LGB population in its April 2013 Universal Periodic Review, contrary to its stance in the 2009 review, during which the foreign minister stated there were no LGB individuals in the country.

Members of LGBTI communities regularly received threatening messages via telephone, text, and social media, and some were harassed by the police. During the Bengali New Year (Pohela Boishakh) celebration, police prevented members of the LGBTI community from participating in a parade, ostensibly to protect them from rumored attacks, by detaining and reportedly humiliating them--including by divulging their LGBTI status to their family members. Following the parade, members of the community reported both online and in person harassment. On April 25, assailants allegedly linked to AQIS killed human rights activist Xulhaz Mannan and his friend Mahbub Rabbi Tonoy in Mannan's home using machetes. The two killings generated a chilling effect within the LGBTI activist community, according to contacts. Following the event and continued harassment, many members of LGBTI communities, including the leadership of key support organizations, reduced their activities and sought refuge both inside and outside of the country. This resulted in severely weakened advocacy and support networks for LGBTI persons. Organizations specifically assisting lesbians continued to be rare. Strong social stigma based on sexual orientation was common and prevented open discussion of the subject.

HIV and AIDS Social Stigma

Social stigma against HIV and AIDS and against higher-risk populations could be a barrier for accessing health services, especially for the transgender community and men who have sex with men. Gender norms sometimes prevented women from accessing HIV information and services. According to the People Living with HIV Stigma Index, HIV-positive persons at times faced social ostracism, detention, and denial of inheritance rights. The overall HIV infection rate was less than 0.1 percent. Funding for HIV projects declined leading to closure of some service centers.

There were limited reports of violence against HIV/AIDS patients. NGOs said this was partly a function of fear if victims identified themselves and an absence of research due to the relatively low rate of HIV/AIDS in the country.

Other Societal Violence or Discrimination

Vigilante killings occurred. Local human rights organizations acknowledged the number of reported cases probably represented only a fraction of the actual incidents. Illegal fatwas and village arbitration, which a prominent local NGO defined as rulings given by community leaders rather than religious scholars, also occurred. In April, villagers in Khulna district assaulted two Hindu teachers for allegedly insulting the Prophet Muhammed and locked them in a school. The teachers were sentenced to six months in prison for "hurting religious sentiments."

Section 7. Worker Rights

a. Freedom of Association and the Right to Collective Bargaining

The law provides for the right to join unions and, with government approval, the right to form a union, although labor rights organizations said that cumbersome requirements for union registration remained. The law requires a minimum of 30 percent of an enterprise's total workforce to agree to be members before the Ministry of Labor and Employment may grant approval for a union, and the ministry may request a court to dissolve the union if membership falls below 30 percent. The law allows only wall-to-wall (entire factory) bargaining units. The labor law definition of workers excludes managerial, supervisory, and administrative staff. Firefighting staff, security guards, and employers' confidential assistants may not join a union. Civil service and security force employees are prohibited from forming unions. The ministry may deregister unions for other reasons with the approval of a labor court. The law affords unions the right of appeal in the cases of dissolution or denial of registration. Export Processing Zones (EPZs), which currently do not allow trade union participation, are a notable exception to the national labor law (see below).

Prospective unions continued to report rejections based on reasons not listed in the labor law. The Ministry of Labor and Employment (MOLE) reports that there are 7,659 trade unions in Bangladesh, covering nearly 3 million workers, with 507 unions in the garment sector, including 375 new unions since 2013. MOLE reported that there were 16 unions in the shrimp sector and 13 unions in the leather and tannery sector. According to the Solidarity Center, a significant number of the unions in the readymade garment (RMG) sector were no longer active during the year due to factory closures or alleged unfair labor practices on the part of employers. After a rise in applications in February, the trade union application rate decreased over the course of the year. MOLE reported a better acceptance rate of RMG unions in Dhaka in the current year than in the prior year, with 52 percent of RMG unions successfully registering compared to 27 percent in 2015. The acceptance rate decreased in Chittagong to 41 percent (11 accepted and 16 rejected as of August) compared to 75 percent in 2015. Notably, the number of unions applying for registration significantly decreased in 2016. According to the Solidarity Center, MOLE had registered 47 RMG unions (36 in Dhaka and 11 in Chittagong) and rejected 41 (24 in Dhaka and 17 in Chittagong) as of December, compared with 61 registrations and 148 rejections in all of 2015. Solidarity Center also reported that 347 RMG factories have unions, and some of these factories have more than one union.

Workers at Dhaka Dyeing Garments attempted to register their union three times. The labor ministry rejected the application twice for what workers said were illegal grounds. After the third registration attempt, Ministry officials visited the factory and allegedly tried to turn workers against the union. Workers also publicly claimed the Joint Director of Labor in Dhaka offered the organizing trade union federation money to cease registration efforts. In November 2015, the employer fired more than 100 workers, workers protested, and the employers closed the factory for an illegal work stoppage, with approval from MOLE. After the factory closure, the federation and owners signed a Memorandum of Agreement, which outlined severance for the workers. In 2016, MOLE transferred the Joint Director of Labor in Dhaka, who faced corruption complaints from federations, to another jurisdiction.

The law provides for the right to conduct legal strikes but with many limitations. For example, the government may prohibit a strike deemed to pose a "serious hardship to the community" and may terminate any strike lasting more than 30 days. The law additionally prohibits strikes for the first three years of commercial production or if the factory was built with foreign investment or owned by a foreign investor. Starting December 11, 59 factories in Ashulia, an industrial suburb of Dhaka, experienced work stoppages when thousands of workers went on strike to demand wage increases. The country's major labor federations did not organize the strike; however, at least 11 labor leaders were detained and arrested by local authorities following the incident for a range of allegations, including charges under the Special Powers Act. Following reported harassment from the industrial police, several labor federations operating in Ashulia and other areas closed their offices, as well as worker community centers supported by the Solidarity Center.

Legally registered unions are entitled to submit charters of demands and bargain collectively with employers; this occurred rarely, but instances were increasing. The law provides criminal penalties for unfair labor practices such as retaliation against union members for exercising their legal rights. Labor organizations reported that in some companies, workers did not exercise their collective bargaining rights due to their unions' ability to address grievances with management informally or due to fear of reprisal. According to the Solidarity Center, as of October, garment sector unions and their management reached 22 collective bargaining agreements in factories with active unions.

Workers seeking to form a union at Reliance Denim Industries Ltd. (Reliance), a factory in Chittagong, were able to address grievances with management following two violent assaults in January. On January 13, 20 men reportedly attacked a union organizer on his way home from a labor-management meeting and the next day 40 men, including a factory manager, attacked employees within the factory. Factory managers blamed union leaders for the attack in the factory, had the organizer arrested and then refused to allow at least seven people to enter the factory on January 16, effectively causing their suspension. After receiving pressure from at least one brand, on January 25, the union reached an agreement with management to drop criminal charges, allow workers to return to the factory with back-pay for time missed, make a statement to the workforce regarding freedom of association, and start regular labor-management meetings.

The law includes provisions protecting unions from employer interference in organizing activities; however, employers, particularly in the readymade garment industry, often interfered with this right. Labor organizers reported acts of intimidation and abuse, the termination of employees, and scrutiny by security forces and the intelligence services. Labor rights NGOs alleged that some terminated union members were unable to find work in the sector because employers blacklisted them. The BGMEA reported that some factory owners complained about harassment from organized labor, including physical intimidation, but statistics and specific examples were unavailable.

Workers at the Azim Group, a Bangladeshi manufacturer operating multiple factories, have met repeated intimidation, retaliation, and physical violence in their efforts to exercise their associational rights. Following violent attacks on union organizers in Azim-owned factories in 2014, workers at three Azim-owned factories worked to form unions affiliated with the Bangladesh Independent Garment Worker Union Federation (BIGUF) in late 2015. Factory managers retaliated by suspending nine workers involved in the organizing effort. The Worker Rights Consortium (WRC) reported that factory managers and supervisors threatened to kill worker activists for organizing a union. On March 31, the JDL rejected all three registration applications with minimal rationale. In May, following intense pressure from buyers contacted by BIGUF and WRC, Azim Group reinstated the nine suspended workers, who have continued their organizing efforts and will refile their applications for union registration.

Managers of Panorama Apparels Ltd. (Panorama) in Gazipur stifled workers' efforts to organize with assistance of local ruling party politicians. According to WRC, management coerced five workers seeking to form a union to resign on February 29 while the JDL reviewed their application. The JDL then rejected the union registration application on suspect grounds, including the fact that the union's President and Secretary did not work at the factory (as management had just coerced them to resign). Following pressure from brands, management agreed to several meetings in April with the union leaders to discuss reinstatement of the five individuals and protection of their right to organize. Using a combination of pressure and intimidation from AL politicians and coercion (e.g., denying union leaders the opportunity to consult legal counsel and presenting them a written agreement in English, which they do not understand), however, management convinced the workers not to return to the factory. MOLE reported that five workers voluntarily quit their jobs at Panorama and received their due compensation; MOLE has reported these complaints resolved.

At Friends Stylewear Ltd., factory management terminated all active union members, and in response to several Unfair Labor Practice complaints, the JDL has filed 18 cases against the factory owner according to the WRC. As of August, the cases are pending in the Labor Court.

According to 2013 Amendments to the labor law, every factory with more than 50 employees is required to have an elected Workers' Participation Committee (WPC). In September 2015, the government passed the Bangladesh Labor Rules called for in the amended law. The rules include an outline of the process for WPC elections. As of August, the government reports that approximately 236 WPCs were formed with the majority in the RMG sector.

A separate legal framework under the authority of the Bangladesh Export Processing Zone (EPZ) Authority (BEPZA) governs labor rights in the EPZs, where approximately 458,000 Bangladeshis work. EPZ law specifies certain limited associational and bargaining rights for Worker Welfare Associations (WWAs) elected by the workers, such as the rights to bargain collectively and represent their members in disputes. According to BEPZA, 231 WWAs were formed as of September. The law prohibits unions within EPZs. While an earlier provision of the EPZ law banning all strikes under penalty of imprisonment expired in 2013, the law continues to provide for strict limits on the right to strike, such as the discretion of the BEPZA's chairman to ban any strike he views as prejudicial to the public interest. The law provides for EPZ labor tribunals, appellate tribunals, and conciliators, but those institutions were not established. Instead eight labor courts and one appellate labor court heard EPZ cases. The BEPZA has its own inspection regime with labor counselors that function as inspectors. WWAs in EPZs are prohibited from establishing any connection to outside political parties, unions, federations, or NGOs.

There were no reports of legal strikes in the EPZs. Parliament continued to defer action on a draft EPZ law, which, along with the Bangladesh Labor Act, does not meet international labor standards according to the ILO. The Parliamentary Standing Committee on Ministry of Law, Justice, and Parliamentary Affairs held several hearings on the draft law, including one on September 29 where the committee solicited feedback from the international community. Following the September 29 meeting, the committee chair assigned a subcommittee the task of reviewing comparable practices in neighboring countries. The committee had not reported back at the end of the year.

With the exception of limitations on the right of association and worker protections in the EPZs, national labor law prohibits antiunion discrimination. A labor court may order the reinstatement of workers fired for union activities, but this right was rarely exercised.

The government did not always enforce applicable law effectively or consistently. For example, labor law establishes mechanisms for conciliation, arbitration, and dispute resolution by a labor court and workers in a collective-bargaining union have the right to strike in the event of a failure to reach a settlement. In practical terms, few strikes followed the cumbersome legal requirements, and strikes or walkouts often occurred spontaneously.

Penalties for violating the law increased in 2013, enabled by the issuance of implementing rules. The maximum fine for a first violation is 25,000 taka ($313); the fine doubles for a second offense. The law also allows for imprisonment of up to three years. If a violation results in death, the law allows a fine of up to 100,000 taka ($1,250), four years' imprisonment, or both. Administrative and judicial appeals were subject to lengthy delays.

b. Prohibition of Forced or Compulsory Labor

The law prohibits all forms of forced or compulsory labor. Penalties for forced or bonded labor offenses are five to 12 years' imprisonment and a fine of not less than 50,000 taka ($625). Inspection mechanisms that enforce laws against forced labor did not function effectively. Resources, inspections, and remediation efforts were inadequate. The law also provides that victims of forced labor have access to shelter and other protective services afforded to trafficking victims.

Some individuals recruited to work overseas with fraudulent employment offers subsequently were exploited abroad under conditions of forced labor or debt bondage. Many migrant workers assume debt to pay high recruitment fees, imposed legally by recruitment agencies belonging to the Bangladesh Association of International Recruiting Agencies (BAIRA) and illegally by unlicensed sub-agents.

Some instances of bonded labor and domestic service were reported, predominately in rural areas. Children and adults were forced into domestic servitude and bonded labor that involved restricted movement, nonpayment of wages, threats, and physical or sexual abuse (see section 7.c.).

See the Department of State's *Trafficking in Persons Report* at www.state.gov/j/tip/rls/tiprpt/.

c. Prohibition of Child Labor and Minimum Age for Employment

The law regulates child employment, and the regulations depend on the type of work and the child's age. The minimum age for work is 14, and the minimum age for hazardous work is 18. The law allows for certain exceptions, permitting children who are ages 12 or 13 to perform restricted forms of light work. Minors can work up to five hours per day and 30 hours per week in factories or up to seven hours per day and 42 per week in other types of workplaces. By law every child must attend school through fifth grade.

The labor Ministry's enforcement mechanisms were insufficient for the large, urban informal sector, and there was little enforcement of child labor laws outside the export-garment and shrimp-processing sectors. Agriculture and other informal sectors that had no government oversight employed large numbers of children.

Under the Ministry's 2012-2016 Child Labor National Plan of Action, the National Child Labor Welfare Council is charged with monitoring child labor. The council has only met twice, however, since its inception. The government mandated child protection networks at district and subdistrict levels to respond to a broad spectrum of violations against children, including child labor; to monitor interventions; and to develop referral mechanisms.

The law specifies penalties for violations involving child labor, including nominal fines of less than 5,000 taka ($63). These penalties were insufficient to deter violations. The government occasionally brought criminal charges against employers who abused domestic servants. MOLE filed 40 child labor cases in 2015; in general, resources, inspections, and remedial action were inadequate.

On July 10, a 10-year-old boy named Sagar Barman was killed at Zobeda Textile and Spinning Mills where he worked with his father. His father accused management in the factory of beating him and killing his son by using an air compressor to pump air into his son's rectum; similar murders occurred in August 2015 and December 2016. The boy's death led to discovery of 24 children working at the factory, aged between 10 and 15 years old. The Department of Inspections of Factories and Establishments (DIFE) reportedly filed a case against the factory in court, and police arrested the supervisor.

Child labor was widespread, particularly in the informal sector and in domestic work. According to a 2016 Overseas Development Institute report based on a survey of 2,700 households in Dhaka's slums, 15 percent of 6- to 14-year-old children were out of school and engaged in full-time work. These children were working well beyond the 42-hour limit set by national legislation. The ready-made garment industry was the main employer of these children and accounted for two thirds of female child labor.

According to the ILO, agriculture is the primary employment sector for boys and services is the main sector for girls. According to the BBS 2015 Bangladesh Child Labor Report, 3.45 million children are working and 1.28 million are employed in hazardous jobs. The BBS estimates that 17.1 percent of working children suffered verbal abuse, 1.2 percent suffered beatings, and 2.5 percent suffered sexual abuse. A recent UNICEF survey in Keranigaj found that 59 percent of an estimated 185,000 workers in the area were under the age of 18 and worked up to 17 hours per day during peak production. According to Young Power in Social Action, an NGO working to protect the rights of shipbreakers in Chittagong, 11 percent of the shipbreaking workforce is under the age of 18. NGOs, such as Shipbreaking Platform, report laborers work long hours without training, safety equipment, holidays, adequate health care, or contractual agreements. At least 16 workers died in the industry in 2015.

Children were engaged in the worst forms of child labor, primarily in dangerous activities in agriculture. Children working in agriculture risked using dangerous tools, carrying heavy loads, and applying harmful pesticides. Children frequently worked long hours, were exposed to extreme temperatures, and suffered high rates of injury from sharp tools. Children also worked in such hazardous activities as stone and brick breaking, dyeing operations, blacksmith assistance, and construction. Forced child labor was present in the fish-drying industry, where children were exposed to harmful chemicals, dangerous machines, and long hours of work. In urban areas, street children work pulling rickshaws, garbage picking, recycling, vending, begging, repairing automobiles, and working in hotels and restaurants. These children were vulnerable to exploitation, for example, in forced begging or being used to smuggle or sell drugs.

Children frequently worked in the informal sector in areas including the unregistered garment, road transport, manufacturing, and service industries.

See the Department of Labor's *Findings on the Worst Forms of Child Labor* at www.dol.gov/ilab/reports/child-labor/findings/.

d. Discrimination with respect to Employment and Occupation

The labor law prohibits wage discrimination on the basis of sex or disability, but it does not prohibit other discrimination based on sex, disability, social status, caste, sexual orientation, or similar factors. The constitution prohibits adverse discrimination by the state on the basis of religion, race, caste, sex, or place of birth and expressly extends that prohibition to government employment; it allows affirmative action programs for the benefit of disadvantaged populations.

The lower-wage garment sector has traditionally offered employment opportunities for women. Women represented the majority of garment sector workers, making up approximately 56 percent of the total RMG workforce according to official statistics although statistics varied widely due to a lack of data. The ILO estimates that women make up 65 percent of the RMG workforce. Despite representing a majority of total workers, women were generally underrepresented in supervisory and management positions. Women were subjected to abuse in factories, including sexual harassment. There were gender-based wage disparities in the overall economy, including in the garment sector.

Some religious, ethnic, and other minorities reported discrimination, particularly in the private sector (see section 6.).

e. Acceptable Conditions of Work

The National Minimum Wage Board established minimum monthly wages on a sector-by-sector basis. The board may convene at any time, but it is supposed to meet at least every five years in a tripartite forum to set wage structures and benefits industry by industry. By law, the government may modify or amend existing wage structures through official public announcement in consultation with employers and workers. In the garment industry, the board set the minimum monthly wage at 5,300 taka ($66) in 2013. Wages in the apparel sector often were higher than the minimum wage, and wages in the EPZs typically were higher than general wage levels--5,500 taka ($70) per month according to BEPZA. Among the lowest minimum wages were those for tea packaging set in 2013 at 69 taka ($0.86) per day established by a Memorandum of Understanding. None of the set minimum wages provided a sufficient standard of living for urban dwellers. The minimum wage was not indexed to inflation (which averaged 7 to 8 percent annually), but the board occasionally made cost-of-living adjustments to wages in some sectors.

By law, a standard workday is eight hours. A standard workweek is 48 hours but may be extended to 60 hours, subject to the payment of an overtime allowance that is double the basic wage. Overtime cannot be compulsory. Workers must have one hour of rest if they work for more than eight hours a day or a half-hour of rest for more than five hours' work a day. Factory workers are supposed to receive one day off every week. Shop workers receive one and one-half days off per week. The law establishes occupational health and safety standards, and recent amendments to the law created mandatory worker safety committees. The law says that every worker should be allowed at least 11 festival holidays with full wages in a year. The days and dates for such festivals may be fixed by the employer.

Labor law implementing rules outline the process for the formation of occupational safety and health (OSH) committees in factories, and the government reports that approximately 133 safety committees were formed as of August. The committees will include both management and workers nominated by the union or the factory's WPC. Where there is no union or WPC, the labor ministry will arrange an election among the workers for their representatives.

The government did not effectively enforce minimum wage, hours of work, and occupational safety and health standards in all sectors. Although increased focus on the garment industry improved compliance in some garment factories, resources, inspections, and remediation were generally not adequate across sectors, and penalties for violations were not sufficient to deter violations.

MOLE resources were inadequate to inspect and remediate problems effectively, and the Ministry lacked authority to sanction employers directly without filing a court case. The Ministry nonetheless took steps to increase its staff and technical capacity. The government increased the Ministry's budget by 370 percent in the 2014-2015 fiscal year and a further 72 percent to $4.1 million in 2015-2016. As of April, the Ministry had 277 active inspectors of which 235 had been hired after Rana Plaza. As of June 2016, MOLE reported it had approval and was in the process of hiring an additional 169 inspectors. The Public Service Commission was in the process of hiring 89 of these new inspectors at the year's end. MOLE reported receiving 66 allegations of anti-union discrimination, of which it resolved 32. The Ministry stated in August that it received approval from the Ministry of Public Administration to upgrade the Directorate of Labor to the Department of Labor, which will increase its staff from 712 to 1,043. The upgrade is now pending approval from the Ministry of Finance.

The 2013 Rana Plaza building collapse killed 1,138 workers and injured more than 2,500. In the aftermath of the collapse, private companies, foreign governments, and international organizations worked with the government to inspect more than 3,660 garment factories, leading to 39 full and 42 partial closures of factories for imminent danger to human life as of August. Many factories began to take action to improve safety conditions, although remediation in many cases has proceeded slowly due to a range of factors, including failure to access adequate financing. The court case against Sohel Rana, the owner of Rana Plaza, and 40 other individuals on charges including murder began on July 18. Witness deposition started on September 18. The trial was ongoing at year's end.

A trial against those implicated in the 2012 Tazreen Fashions fire started on January 9 after charges were brought against 13 people, including chairman Mahmuda Akhter and managing director Delwar Hossain, in September 2015. Media reported that the trial was stalled at the end of the year.

Workers' groups stated that OSH standards established by law were sufficient and that more factories took steps toward compliance. The law provides for a maximum fine of 25,000 taka ($313) for noncompliance, but this did not deter violations.

Legal limits on hours of work were violated routinely. In the RMG sector, employers often required workers to labor 12 hours a day or more to meet export deadlines, but they did not always properly compensate workers for their time. According to the Solidarity Center, workers often willingly worked overtime in excess of the legal limit. Employers commonly delayed workers' pay or denied full leave benefits. Labor Ministry inspections did not report any overtime violations.

Safety conditions at many workplaces were extremely poor, but the Solidarity Center and others reported significant safety improvements in the RMG sector. The Bangladesh Fire Service and Civil Defense upgraded its inspection unit from 55 to 265 inspectors, who received training on developing fire safety management plans for fire, building and electrical issues in garment factories. Formal sector factories outside of the RMG industry remain largely outside the scope of safety inspectors. On September 10, an explosion and fire at Tampaco Foils factory in Gazipur killed 35 people, demonstrating continued shortcomings in safety and proper facilities oversight despite improvements made since the Rana Plaza disaster.

Few reliable labor statistics were available on the large informal sector in which the majority of citizens worked, and it was difficult to enforce labor laws in the sector. The BBS 2010 Labor Force Survey reported the informal sector employed 47.3 million of the 56.7 million workers in the country.